The Blueprint for Bliss

Scientific and Spiritual Keys to a Happy Life

By
Richard Gibson

Copyright 2024 Richard Gibson. All rights reserved.

No part of this book may be reproduced in any form or by any electronic or mechanical means including information storage and retrieval systems, without permission in writing from the author. The only exception is by a reviewer, who may quote short excerpts in a review.

Although the author and publisher have made every effort to ensure that the information in this book was correct at press time, the author and publisher do not assume and hereby disclaim any liability to any party for any loss, damage, or disruption caused by errors or omissions, whether such errors or omissions result from negligence, accident, or any other cause.

This publication is designed to provide accurate and authoritative information concerning the subject matter covered. It is sold with the understanding that the publisher does not render professional services. If legal advice or other expert assistance is required, the services of a competent professional should be sought.

The fact that an organisation or website is referred to in this work as a citation and/or a potential source of further information does not mean that the author or the publisher endorses the information the organisation or website may provide or recommendations it may make.

Please remember that Internet websites listed in this work may have changed or disappeared between when this work was written and when it was read.

Cover designed by Get Covers

This book is dedicated to shining a light on those who may feel lost or overlooked, reminding them that their presence and purpose are valuable and meaningful.
I see you

Contents

Preface 1
Prologue 2
Introduction 5
Chapter 1: The Foundation to Bliss 7
Chapter 2: Mastering Breathwork 17
Chapter 3: The Power of Meditation 28
Chapter 4: Conducting a Health Check 39
Chapter 5: Nourishment for Happiness 56
Chapter 6: Enhancing Life Through Sleep 65
Chapter 7: Discovering Purpose 75
Chapter 8: Rewiring Subconscious Beliefs 84
Chapter 9: Integrating Body, Mind, and Spirit 98
Chapter 10: Cultivating Self Love 108
Chapter 11: The Gratitude Attitude 118
Chapter 12: Do Not Worry, Be Happy 127
Chapter 13: Living the Blueprint for Bliss 138
About the Author 142
Appendix 144

Preface

Most will agree that when it comes to life, quality is far more important than quantity. Yet we miss the quality every day. Quality of life comes from being present and enjoying the moment. All that matters is here and now. Without presence, there is no quality. You may feel that this quality is out of reach, but relax; I am here to help. You are on your way to that quality of life you seek. It has many steps, but each step makes life more enjoyable.

There is a Japanese word, "Kaizen", which means continuous and constant improvement. Subscribe to this to improve your life continuously and constantly.

Prologue

My life started out pretty standard, so I thought. It turns out, early on things were going south; I just couldn't see it.

By my early 40s, I was divorced, and with no contact with my four children, I was crushed. My bank account was empty; I had to walk away from the company I co-founded. I hit rock bottom. I started again, but my mindset was the same, and eight years later, I found myself ending another relationship with a dearly loving partner. I lost my home, and crippling bills left me unable to afford rent or a mortgage.

At the age of 47, I was reliant on the charity of my family, or I literally would have been on the street.

This all could be blamed on others, but the reality is that my own poor choices brought me here.

Don't get me wrong; I have always acted with integrity despite being faced with strong opposition from those who lack it.

The Blueprint for Bliss

I didn't always know something was wrong. It took a great many years to see the impending train wreck, and even then, it took many more years to understand there was change required.

I was always of the opinion that I was the one in control. Turns out that part was correct. Others can provide help. But only I could fix myself. Trouble is when you are really hurting, you don't want to be the one to rely on.

I felt alone and isolated. I had people that loved me deeply, but they did not understand what I was going through. I thought I was the only one whose biggest enemy was inside their head. I was trapped in a mental hell.

It turns out many people feel or have felt like I did. This is why this book exists.

I spent a decade knowing there was nothing at all ok about my normal, and I spent those years in a desperate search for answers. The answers were easy to come by, but unfortunately, it took a lot of sifting to remove the noise. The more significant issue was that my demons were multi-faceted, requiring different angles of attack.

The answers lay in nuggets across many books, but I hope to apply the critical points of many sources here to cut down your search time.

If you are hurting right now. I encourage you to stay strong. This book is not a quick fix. You will need to work. And you will need to make some changes.

This is an overhaul of mind, body and spirit. You do not need to do everything, but the more you embrace, the faster and more effective your results could be.

Your best is yet to come.

Introduction

Welcome to the gateway of your next big adventure – the grand journey towards living your best life. Now, I know that might sound like a hefty promise, a towering order of the tallest sort. But let me assure you, this isn't just another self-help spiel that leaves you flexing your happiness muscles in front of a mirror, hoping for a transformative wink from the universe. No siree, we're diving deep, and we've got science, spirit, and a sprinkle of sass to guide us through.

Think of this book as your all-access pass to the concert of your life - where you're not just in the audience, but the star act, the headliner. That's right; we're cranking up the volume on your potential and lighting up the stage for an encore-worthy performance in the art of living blissfully.

Before we stride forth towards chapters filled with wisdom nuggets and life hacks, let's take a moment to talk about what you won't find here. There will be no labyrinthine jargon that makes you feel like you're decoding an ancient scroll. No unreachable standards have you chasing after a bliss that's forever just one self-improvement book away. Can you feel that? That's the weight of expectations dropping off your shoulders.

Look at this not just as a book but as a companion, a chatty guide that's been through the highs and lows and is all about sharing that cumulative wisdom with you. So, put on your explorer's hat, adjust your curiosity goggles, and let's embark on a riveting escapade that's all about celebrating the brilliant, beautiful life you deserve. Ready to turn the page? Let's do this!

Chapter 1:
The Foundation to Bliss

So, let's dive heart-first into what you're here for: building the foundation for a blissed-out existence. Imagine our lives are like houses, and before we start slapping on some bold-coloured paint or hanging those twinkly lights, we gotta make sure that the foundation is rock-solid. Now, I'm not about to throw a load of bricks and mortar at you; nah, we're talking about the blueprint of your very own joy palace.

Before we even whisper about breathwork or meditate on, well, meditation, let's talk groundwork. It's that unsexy but oh-so-crucial foundation. Think about it – if your smile isn't built on something sturdy, it will wobble faster than a Jenga tower at a toddler's birthday party. And while it might sound like a tall order, I promise you, this is where the magic starts – where science shakes hands with spirituality, and we start sketching out the grand plans for your best life. So, grab your hard hat (just kidding, wear whatever makes you feel fabulous), and let's get to building!

Understanding the Blueprint

Might sound like you're about to tackle a complex architectural drawing, but we're discussing something more exciting and personal: the master plan for your best life. Imagine this blueprint as less about rigid steel beams and more about guidelines sketched in the sand. It's a map of sorts, fine-tuned by your own footsteps as you journey through it.

The essence of any blueprint lies in its details—yet for your best life, these aren't measured in inches or feet but in moments and feelings. The biggest misconception? That this blueprint is universal. Spoiler alert: it's not. Everyone's blueprint is unique and tailored to individual aspirations, values, and quirks. Yes, quirks—we're keeping it real because perfection is the killer of joy and, frankly, quite boring.

So, how does one decode this intriguing, personal blueprint, you ask? It starts with self-awareness. You can't build the house of dreams without knowing what rooms you need, right? This is internal groundwork, a foundational step omitted from too many life plans that causes them to crumble when the winds pick up.

It's key to understand that observing your blueprint is not a passive activity. Bringing it to life involves probing questions, sometimes uncomfortable ones. What makes you tick? And conversely, what completely grinds your gears? Jot these down if you have to—yes, pen and paper style. You might surprise yourself with what flows out.

Consider the values of your blueprint's building codes—they are your non-negotiables. If you're sketching out your blueprint and notice it's missing humour, adventure, or connection, and those matter to you, it's time to redraw some lines. For some, happiness lives in the expanse of open space; for others, in the cosy nooks.

Your blueprint also allows room for revisions and extensions. As you grow, it does too. So, if you suddenly find yourself passionate about underwater basket weaving, by all means, add that annex. There's no "You Are Here" sign on this journey. You get to move and shake it as you see fit.

Blueprints are also known for their durability. Your path to bliss will likely include a few storms. Understanding your blueprint means recognising its resilience—you've got what it takes to get back up, even when life has other plans. This resilience doesn't come from the lines on the blueprint itself. Instead, it's etched from the mindset you bring to the drafting table. When faced with challenges, will you choose to see them as opportunities for a new addition or as flaws in the design?

The joy of this blueprint? It's wonderfully eco-friendly! It only uses the energy you put into it, and believe it or not, the more positivity you pour in, the more sustainable it becomes. It's about building something thriving, not just surviving.

Moving forward with your blueprint in hand—or mind, rather—requires a hefty dose of trust. Trust in the unknown. Trust in the process. Trust that even on days when you feel like giving in to the siren call of settling for less, your blueprint—your plan for your best life—is worth the effort.

Understanding the blueprint also means embracing flexibility. Life is the ultimate improvisation master. Sometimes, it throws in a surprise scene or a plot twist. Don't panic. Breathe. It's just another chance to dance, to adapt your blueprint on the fly.

Let's talk about the fun part: customisation. Sprinkle in those personal touches that only you can add. Maybe you're all about those early morning "I've conquered the world before breakfast" vibes, or perhaps your blueprint includes daily siestas. No judgment. It's your deal, your rules.

It's also vital to remember that some days, you'll kill it out there. Your blueprint will shine, and you'll follow it to a T. On other days, it might as well be written in invisible ink. That's okay, too. It's part of the human package—ups, downs, and all the sidewinders in between.

Even though we're talking about a personal blueprint for bliss, it's not a solitary venture. Interaction is key. Shared laughter, shared tears, and shared wisdom often add colour where you least expect it. Reach out, connect, and embrace the helpers, the mentors, and the friends who contribute to the vitality of your plan.

As you meticulously—or not so meticulously—work on understanding your blueprint, remember that it doesn't need to be perfect. It's a reflection of you in all your evolving, glorious complexity. Revisit it, revise it, revel in it.

In the grand scheme of things, this blueprint journey is meant to be savoured, not rushed. Each step, turn, and hopscotch is a testament to your willingness to create your version of the best life. So, take the time to study your blueprint. Get to know its quirky edges, its bold strokes, and its whispered secrets. After all, it's more than just a plan; it's the art of crafting your joy, one heartful moment at a time.

Science Meets Spirituality: Unifying Principles

Welcome back to the journey where we bridge the gap between two realms that often seem oceans apart:

Science and spirituality. Some say they're like oil and water, but I'm here to show you they've been doing a cosmic tango all along. So hang onto your atoms and your chakras alike—we're about to get unified!

Let's talk cosmic cookies. Imagine science as this delectable, logical cookie—crisp on the edges with well-baked facts. Spirituality, on the other hand, is the gooey centre, resonating with intuition and a sense of oneness. Now, what's life without a full cookie? We can't just live on the edges or the centre alone, right? That's where our unifying principles come into the picture, mixing both to create a scrumptious life experience.

Digging into quantum physics, you'll find it's not just about particles and waves but about potentiality and connectedness. That's pretty spiritual if you ask me! Quantum entanglement shows us that particles, once intertwined, can affect each other across vast distances. Doesn't that sound a lot like the spiritual concept of interconnectedness? It's like everyone and everything in the universe swapping text messages on a cosmic WhatsApp group.

Now let's talk vibes—vibrations if we're being sciencey. Good vibes are not just a hip thing but a literal concept where everything vibrates at its own frequency. Science shows us through cymatics how sound frequencies can create patterns in matter. Spirituality nods in agreement and reminds us that 'tuning into' good vibes is like finding your favourite radio station—except it's the frequency of joy, love, and peace.

And if you think about the chaos theory, where small changes can have enormous impacts, you're basically describing the Butterfly Effect. It's intriguingly similar to the spiritual law of cause and effect, or karma. One little flutter of kindness or positivity can set off a hurricane of goodwill in the world. Who knew butterflies and physicists would get along so well?

Here's something else they agree on: the observer effect. Science tells us that the act of observing a particle can change its behaviour. Similarly, spiritually speaking, where you place your attention expands in your life. If you're constantly observing negativity, you might just find it at every corner. Conversely, focus on the good stuff, and voila! More good stuff seems to magnetically drift your way like leaves to a whirlwind.

Get this: neuroplasticity! It's not just a funky term but the brain's ability to change and adapt. Meditate, and bam—you're rewiring your brain for peace and happiness, according to science. And spirituality has been promoting this for millennia through practices like meditation and mindfulness. It's like your brain is the ultimate Play-Doh.

Now, let's step into the realm of biology. Our bodies, these marvellous wonders, are ecosystems of cells, bacteria, and biochemical reactions that work in a harmonious symphony—most of the time. That's Mother Nature's design, and guess what? Sustainability, interdependence, and balance are core spiritual beliefs too. It's like Mother Nature is the OG spiritual guru, whispering life tips through her creations.

How about the concept of energy conservation? Energy cannot be created or destroyed; it merely transforms. We see this in science with the law of conservation of energy and in spirituality with the concept of eternal souls transitioning through different states. Whether you're analysing thermodynamics or pondering reincarnation, you're appreciating the cycle of transformation—a celestial recycling program, if you will.

Switching gears to the placebo effect, it's not just for sugar pills and snake oil. The power of belief can physically alter our bodies. Faith, a foundation in many spiritual traditions, turns out to have tangible, measurable effects. Science confirms that a hopeful heart can be the best medicine. Maybe faith isn't just for the spiritually inclined but also for cellular biologists!

When we look at the dark matter filling our universe, it's akin to the spiritual principle of the unknown and unseen forces at play. There's comfort in knowing that both scientists and spiritual teachers honour the mystery and acknowledge there's so much more beyond our current understanding. Every time science uncovers a new piece of the universe's puzzle, spirituality nods sagely and says, 'I knew you had it in you!'.

We've all heard of the Golden Ratio, this magical number permeating nature, art, and architecture. It's the universe's preferred scale of balance and proportion, a testament to the inherent synergy in all things. That's mathematical poetry for you, echoing the spiritual pursuit of harmony and balance. Nature's aesthetics are no accident; they're coded into the very fabric of life, much like how we strive for balance in our soulful endeavours.

Let's not forget mindfulness, a trendy topic bridging science and spirituality with style. Mindfulness training, rooted in ancient spiritual practice, now stars in cutting-edge clinical research for reducing stress and enhancing overall well-being. Science confirms that living in the now isn't just a spiritual catchphrase—it's verifiable, replicable and incredibly beneficial.

Last but never least, let's talk about the Big Bang, the grand cosmic kickoff. This might be the meet-cute story of science and spirituality—a single point of infinite density exploding into everything we know. For spiritual enthusiasts, it's the universe manifesting itself. For scientists, it's the working model of our cosmos' origin. Different languages, same storybook wonder.

So you see, science and spirituality are not rivals; they're dance partners stepping to the same universal beat. They each offer a lens to view the wonder that is our existence, providing the principles that unite us in a deep understanding of ourselves and the world around us. Keep dancing with both, and you might just find yourself waltzing into a life that's perfectly in tune—a blissful symphony composed by the cosmos, played by you.

Chapter 2:
Mastering Breathwork

Yes, we all know how to breathe to survive, but most of us are not breathing effectively. Poor breathing habits can contribute directly to health issues and also affect our mood.

To compound the issue, stress, fear and anxiety can cause us to slow our breathing dramatically, breathe shallowly and even hold our breath. This can result in low blood oxygen levels and increased blood pressure. Both of these states can put a strain on our organs. Research has shown (cite: psychologytoday.com) that the majority of us (maybe as much as 80%) unconsciously hold our breaths while concentrating on responding to an email or writing a text. This is known as email apnoea or screen apnoea.

So, we've laid the groundwork for reaching our bliss in the first chapter, folks! Now, let's gear up to harness the power of your breath—trust me, it's a game-changer. Think about it: your breath is the loyal buddy that's been with you from the moment you first gasped air, yet we often take it for granted, like background elevator music. But let's crank up the volume on that music and really tune in, shall we? Mastering breathwork isn't just some new-age fad—it's your all-access pass to calming the chaos in your mind and untangling the knots in your body. **We're diving deep into breath control**, and I'm not talking about just breathing in and out like a tired asthmatic pug. We're going to explore techniques that can clear your mind faster than a fresh eraser on a math mistake. And by the time we reach the *advanced twirls and swirls* of breathing, you'll be navigating stressful situations with the grace of a Zen master in a bumper car arena. So, get ready to take the driver's seat in this breath-controlled rollercoaster—we're about to inject some serious clarity and calm into your life.

The Basics of Breath Control

So, we've laid the groundwork, explored the science having a grand ol' time, and now it's time to dive into the life-changing magic of breathing correctly. It's about to get really real, or should I say, really relaxed. You've got the power to shape your own bliss tucked right under your nose. Well, actually, it involves the nose – and also the lungs, diaphragm, and whatnot. But enough with the anatomy class; let's talk control.

The Blueprint for Bliss

You might be thinking, "Hey, I breathe all the time. I'm pretty pro at it." Sure, you're breathing, but are you controlling that breath to channel its full potential? Think about this: every emotion comes with its own breathing pattern. Panic speeds it up, and calmness slows it down. What if you could reverse engineer that process?

Starting with the basics, how do you breathe? If you're sucking in air like a vacuum cleaner going after those last crumbs of chips, we're going to need to tweak that. Aim for the gut, not the chest. Diaphragmatic breathing is the superstar here. Your diaphragm isn't just a fun word from biology class; it's your breath's best buddy. When it drops, your lungs have more space to fill up, and that's what we're aiming for – deep, full breaths that scream chill vibes.

Let's take a deep breath together – go on, a real one. Feel the air travelling down, your stomach rising, not just your chest puffing out. There, you're doing it! Keep practising this; it's like building a muscle, but instead of lifting weights, you're lifting your mood and energy.

Next, we've got pacing. Life's not always a race, and your breathing shouldn't be either. Slow and steady wins the... calmness? Anyway, the point is that learning to regulate the pace of your breath can have massive payoffs. We're talking about fighting off the nasty stress monster and inviting in the cool breeze of calm.

But how slow is slow, you ask? Try the 4-7-8 technique. Inhale on a count of 4, hold for 7, then whoosh, that breath out for 8. This isn't just some random number game; this little sequence is a cheat code for relaxation. Give it a whirl when the walls of life feel like they're closing in; you'll be amazed at how it can expand your personal space.

The fun doesn't stop there. Consistency is your new BFF when it comes to breathwork. Sporadic breaths are like bad Wi-Fi – unreliable and super frustrating. Instead, find a rhythm that's like your favourite chill playlist, and stick to it. Breathing exercises are less of a chore and more like treats for your soul. Yes, you're allowed to have those.

But let's get a bit scientific for a second. Regular, controlled breathing does wonders for the nervous system. It tells your body, "Hey, we're cool here, no lions to run from." When your nervous system gets the memo, it shifts gears from fight-or-flight to rest-and-digest. That means less stress, better digestion, and an all-around happier you. Yay, science!

Sure, mastering breath control won't solve all your life's puzzles, but it sure gives you a steady hand while you're piecing them together. Use it as a tool when life throws you curveballs. Someone cut you off in traffic? Breaths in, smiles out. Spilled coffee on your white shirt? Inhale the calm, exhale the stains.

And here's the thing: you don't need a fancy cushion or a tranquil mountain retreat to get your breath on. You can practice anytime, anywhere. Stuck in a meeting that's dragging longer than a sloth on a stroll? Breathe. Standing in the longest grocery line known to humankind? Breathe. It's like having a secret weapon of serenity in your back pocket.

Now, tie it all together with intention. Remember why you're doing this – to live your best life. With every inhale, visualise drawing in positivity and energy. With every exhale, picture releasing the stress and negativity. Paint your life's canvas with the strokes of intentional breath.

Feeling overwhelmed with the thought of adding another "must-do" to your day? Don't even sweat it. Start small. Tack on a minute of focused breathing before your morning coffee or after you park at work. Tiny moments make big waves.

Before we move on to the fancy stuff in "Advanced Techniques for Clarity and Calm," let's recap, shall we? Breathe with your diaphragm, not just your chest. Pace yourself – slow and steady. Be consistent, like that favourite song you play on repeat. Show your nervous system some love. Use breathwork as your all-day, everyday peace potion.

Armed with the basics of breath control, you're ready to turn the ordinary act of breathing into an extraordinary tool for living your best life. Take these beginner steps, practice them until they're as natural as scrolling through your phone, and watch as the world opens up with a big, relaxing sigh. Trust me, your body, mind, and spirit will thank you for it.

Advanced Techniques for Clarity and Calm

So, you've been practising your breathwork, right? Inhale, exhale, feeling a bit more zen with every breath – superb stuff! But let's be real, sometimes life cranks up the volume and that neat little breathing exercise feels like it's just barely scratching the surface. Relax, you've come to the right place! Let's dig into some advanced techniques that will transform that whisper of calm into a roar.

Now, before we dive in, let's clear something up. Advanced doesn't mean difficult or complex; it's all about deepening the practices you already know and love, and maybe adding a little spice. So let's get to it and talk about breathing patterns. You've got your basic rhythmic ones down, but let's play with the tempo. The 4-7-8 technique is like a lullaby for your nervous system! Four seconds to inhale, hold that breath for seven, and then a luxurious eight-second exhale. Do it right, and you'll feel like you've hit the mute button on the world's craziness.

Moving on, visualisation can take your breathwork to the next level. Envision that with each breath, you're pulling in a sense of peace, right to your core. And with every out-breath, you're booting out stress like it's last season's fashion. It's about getting super vivid with your imagery – think high definition, 4K, the works!

And hey, don't overlook the power of sound. Ever heard of mantras? These are like your breathwork's backup singers, adding depth and resonance to your practice. Pick a word or phrase that feels calming to you – it could be 'peace,' 'joy,' or 'the boss forgot to call a Monday meeting.' Repeat it silently in your head to the rhythm of your breath, and watch the calm roll in like the tide.

It's great that you've made friends with stillness, but let's turn up the heat a bit. Movement can be meditative, too. Ever tried Qi Gong or Tai Chi? These aren't your average workouts. They're like a dance where every move is smoothed out by the breath, marrying movement and mindfulness into a waltz of well-being.

And while we're bending and swaying, don't forget about yoga. Those twists and stretches aren't just for showing off on Instagram; they're designed to release the tension that's cramping your style – and your mind. So hit the mat, connect with your breath, and to answer that age-old question – yes, that pose does look good on you.

What's that I hear? You want something a bit more esoteric, a touch mystical? Enter stage left: mudras. These hand gestures aren't just elaborate ways to impress your friends at parties. They're symbols that can shape your energy flow and deepen your focus during breathwork. Give 'em a try, and you might just unlock a new level of tranquillity.

But don't think it's all about sitting and being statuesque. Let's bring some dynamic breathwork into the mix. You've got your steady, calming breaths, sure. But how about stoking the inner fire with some kapalabhati or "breath of fire"? It's like taking your lungs to the gym – a series of quick, powerful exhales that can torch anxiety and light up your energy.

Breath of Fire is a potent breathing exercise. that can enhance your well-being. Let's explore how to practice it correctly:

1. **Start in a Seated Position**:

Sit cross-legged with your spine straight. Place your hands on your knees with palms facing up. You can also put a hand on your stomach to feel it rise with your breath.

2. **Inhale Passively**:

   Take a deep breath in through your nose, allowing your lungs to fill up with fresh air while your abdomen expands and contracts naturally.

3. **Forceful Exhalation**:

   Without pausing, exhale forcefully through your nose. Contract your abdominal muscles during the exhale.

4. **Maintain the Rhythm**:

   Continue the pattern: passive inhale, forceful exhale. Ensure the inhale and exhale are of equal length, without any pauses in between.

5. **Speed It Up**:

   Start slowly if you're new to this technique. Gradually increase the speed of your breath, maintaining the rhythm.

6. **Duration**: You can practice Breath of Fire for The time required for completion of the task may vary from 30 seconds up to 10 minutes,

depending on your level of experience and personal preference..

Remember, Breath of Fire is a form of pranayama (breath control) commonly done in Kundalini yoga. It offers benefits such as stress reduction, improved respiratory function, and strengthened abdominal muscles.

Okay, quick sidebar for the sceptics – props can help. No, not the kind you get on stage. I'm talking about comfortable cushions, blankets, and maybe even a weighted blanket if you really want to turn it up a notch. They set the scene for serenity and tell your body, "Hey, we're in chill mode now."

Let's not forget the senses. Aromatherapy, anyone? A few spots of lavender or peppermint oil can bridge the gap between 'I'm barely keeping it together' and 'I'm the poster child for zen.' It's amazing what a little olfactory intervention can do for your calm quotient.

And one for the road, because who doesn't love a grand finale? The power nap. That's right, I said it – naps! But not just any old snooze on the couch. I'm talking about a strategic, timed-for-perfection, premeditation power nap. Breathe deeply, set a timer for 20 minutes, and let yourself drift into that sweet spot between wakefulness and sleep. It's like hitting the refresh button in your brain.

The Blueprint for Bliss

Now, before you go off exploring these techniques like a kid in a calmness candy store, remember the golden rule: be consistent. Whether it's breath of fire or meditative napping, practice makes perfect. You're building mental muscle here – the more you flex it, the stronger it gets.

Lastly, remember that your journey to inner calm is as unique as your favourite pair of socks. Mix and match these advanced breathwork techniques until you find the combo that makes you feel like you've got an inner peace generator humming away inside you. Trial and error is the bread and butter of personal growth – and, let's be honest, it's also half the fun!

So there you have it – a menu of advanced techniques to cultivate clarity and calm like you're the master chef of your mind. Savour the process, experiment with flavours, and remember that every breath is a new opportunity to add a dash more serenity to the dish that is your life.

Now, don't go hoarding all this calm to yourself! Share the love, spread the practices, because let's face it – the world could use a tad more tranquillity. May your breaths be deep, your naps be power-packed, and your days be as calm as a zen master who's just won the lottery. Namaste, my friend, and enjoy the journey!

Chapter 3:
The Power of Meditation

Having played around with breathwork, we're now steering into the serene waters of meditation. Picture this: your mind is a bustling metropolis, thoughts zooming around like cars in rush hour—you need that calming traffic light, and meditation is your green, yellow, and red all wrapped into one. It's about tapping into a part of yourself that's been patiently waiting while you've been out there juggling life's curveballs. It's not just about sitting cross-legged and trying not to think for a few minutes (although that's part of the fun); it's unlocking the door to your internal wisdom—like finding cheat codes to your own psyche.

Meditation is that secret sauce, giving your mind the space to simmer down and your spirit the clarity to shine. So, let's dive headfirst into shaping a daily zen ritual that feels like you're treating yourself to a mental spa day, every day, minus the eye-watering bill. Sink into the cushion, let your breath be your anchor, and discover meditative paths that lead to that sweet inner peace—you'll probably find that it's more addictive than the last season of that show you binge-watched!"

Cultivating a Daily Practice

Isn't about setting up camp in the Himalayas or morphing into a serene, robe-wearing sage—it's about integrating simple yet powerful rituals into your everyday hustle. Imagine it as adding a pinch of mindfulness to your morning joe, a splash of tranquillity in your daily commute, and a dash of serenity before hitting the sack. So, grab your internal gardening tools; we're about to cultivate some seriously blissful habits.

Let's kick things off with consistency—your new best friend and the backbone of any successful daily practice. Sure, it sounds about as thrilling as watching paint dry, but hear me out. Consistency is the secret sauce that transforms 'tried once at a retreat' into 'wow, I can actually keep my cool in bumper-to-bumper traffic.' Starting small is key. Choose one practice, like a one-minute morning meditation, and do it every single day. Yes, including when your bed feels like a cloud and the outside world resembles a frozen tundra.

Now, your environment plays a massive role too. You don't need an altar or a Zen garden—unless that's your thing—but carving out a nook for your practice can work wonders. It could be as simple as a comfortable chair near a window or a corner with a mat and your favourite plant. This space doesn't just whisper; it yells, "It's 'me-time', folks!" every time you glance in its direction.

But, ah, the pesky mind - always chatting about this or that. When it comes to meditation or any focus-based practice, expect your mind to act like a hyper puppy—adorable but distracting. Here's where the beauty of gentle redirection comes in. Each time your thoughts wander to grocery lists or that funny meme, gently bring your focus back, no self-judgment allowed. It's not about silencing the mind; it's about becoming a friendly observer.

Let's talk about the power of habits. Hooking your new practice onto an existing habit is like giving it a free piggyback ride. Do you brush your teeth every morning? Perfect, stack your one-minute meditation right before or after. It's about creating a trigger that says, "Teeth are sparkling, time to calm the mind." This is how micro-practices can eventually become second nature.

So, you missed a day? Or three? No sweat. This isn't about perfect attendance awards. The significant part is bouncing back. Don't waste time beating yourself up; redirect that energy into getting back on the mindful bandwagon. Flexibility and self-compassion are essential ingredients in this growth recipe.

While we're on the subject of flexibility, let's talk variety. Just as your taste buds desire an assortment of flavours, your practice could benefit from different spices. Mix it up with breathwork some days, light stretching or a gratitude minute on others. Variation can keep things fresh and engaging, which is a huge plus for preventing the notorious practice doldrums.

Now, if you're the kind who thrives on accountability, get yourself a practice buddy or join a community. Knowing you're not alone in the quest to cultivate zen-like daily habits can be a turbo-boost, especially when motivation wanes. A quick check-in with your buddy or group can rekindle that inner fire on the days it starts to dim.

But let's not forget the 'why' behind your practice. Reflect on how these small daily rituals improve your overall vibe. Has your patience grown? Are you sleeping better? Keeping your 'why' close protects your practice from becoming another mindless checkbox on your to-do list.

Here's a curveball: infuse playfulness into your practice. The moment this all starts to feel like homework is the moment you'll start finding excuses to skip it. So, play with it! Sometimes you'll dive deep, and other times you'll barely skim the surface—and that's perfectly okay. Your practice should bring joy, not feel like another chore to dread.

Let's not ignore the digital elephant in the room: technology. It can be both a tool and a tyrant. Sure, apps that nudge you toward mindfulness are fantastic, but be mindful of becoming too reliant. Balance is everything. Use the tech to support you, not define you.

We often talk about mindfulness in terms of sitting still, but active mindfulness practices can be just as transformative. Walk to the rhythm of your breath, do the dishes with full intention, and savour each mouthful during lunch without the distraction of screens. These are the Zen master moves of modern life.

Patience, my friend. Evolution, not revolution, is the name of the game. Give yourself time to adjust, learn, and gently nudge your boundaries. You're not chasing an endpoint—you're embracing a journey of continuous growth. Celebrate the small victories, like remembering to take a deep breath during a tense moment. These are the real gold stars!

Lastly, bring some rituals to your practice. Light a candle, ring a bell, or play a particular song to signal the beginning and end of your practice time. This sets a clear distinction, a sort of opening and closing ceremony for your daily ritual. It's simple, sure, but the subconscious loves a good ritual. It firmly plants the idea that 'this is important' into your psyche.

Remember, these aren't tasks to conquer; think of them as seeds to nurture. Water them with consistency, give them the light of your attention, and occasionally prune away distractions. Cultivating a daily practice is the art of tending to your inner garden. And guess what? Even on the days when it feels like nothing's blooming, just by showing up, you've planted something extraordinary. Keep nurturing it, and the growth will show, sometimes in the most unexpected and delightful ways.

Meditative Paths to Inner Peace

Let's take a leisurely stroll down the winding path of meditation, shall we? I think you're going to enjoy this part. Imagine meditation as a buffet of delectable options for calming that busy bee buzzing in your bonnet - your mind that is. There's a dish here for every preference, and guess what? No calories involved, only sweet peace of mind.

First up, we've got the classic: mindfulness meditation. It's like your grandma's apple pie – it never goes out of style. Mindfulness asks you to sit down, breathe, and pay close attention to your present moment without any judgment. You're not trying to clear the mind; you're noticing it, working with it, feeling that breath go in and out like the tides. Just when you think you can't possibly focus any longer on your breath, you're already three breaths deep and in the zone. That's mindfulness for you – sneakily effective.

Did someone say movement? Not all meditation requires sitting still like a statue. In fact, walking meditation turns your daily stroll into a mobile Zen adventure. You're not just walking; you're walking with intention, with feeling, with an awareness that each step is a symphony of movement that keeps you grounded and centred. Who knew walking the dog could be so profound?

Let's not forget about guided meditations, the audio books of inner peace. Pop in those earbuds, and let a soothing voice shepherd you through a forest of tranquillity or maybe even a beach of serenity. Neighbour's dog won't stop yapping? No problem. You're on a mental beach, and the only barking you hear is the call of blissful waves.

The Blueprint for Bliss

Moving on, we've got loving-kindness meditation. Forget about kissing frogs; this is where you mentally send out positive vibes to your friends, your foes, and everyone in between. It's like writing Valentine's cards in your mind, spreading the love one thought at a time until your heart feels as light as a helium balloon.

But hey, what about those who find peace in believing something greater than themselves? Enter spiritual meditation. Tracing back to various religious traditions, it's like linking arms with the universe (or God, or the Force, or whatever tickles your cosmic fancy) and harmonising with the great unknown. It's a soulful hum, a connection that makes you feel part of the grand tapestry of life, thread by glorious thread.

So, you've got an artistic side? Then maybe you'll pirouette right over to creative meditations. These aren't just about 'ohmm-ing' in a quiet room; they're about stirring the pot of creativity and cooking up a gastronomic feast with the ingredients of your imagination. Paint a stroke of peace, dance a step of tranquillity, write a script of serenity. Suddenly, your creative block is just another step toward enlightenment.

For the pragmatic folks, perhaps Transcendental Meditation is more your speed. It's like the Tesla of meditations—silent, efficient, and with a hint of celebrity endorsement. You get yourself a personalised mantra, a comfy spot to sit, and twenty minutes later, you're refreshed. It's not hocus-pocus; it's a respite for the thinkers, the achievers, the ones who juggle life like it's hot potatoes.

But wait, there's more! Chakra meditation takes you on a tour of your body's energy centres. Like checking the batteries on your remote, it ensures every spot is charged and ready to go. You'll be aligning energy from head to toe, and maybe bumping into some spiritual blockages on the way. Don't worry, you'll move past them with the grace of a gazelle.

If sitting still truly isn't your style, there's always Kundalini yoga. It's meditation that's not afraid to break a sweat. It's where posture, breath, and focus come together in a fitness trio that leaves you feeling like you've done your body and mind some serious good.

Next, the brainy types might appreciate the challenge of vipassana meditation. It's a bit like a mental marathon – a test of endurance, observation, and getting real cosy with the inner workings of your psyche. You're bound to dig up some interesting finds in this archaeological dig of the mind.

Can't forget about mantra meditation. Much like your favourite catchy tune, a mantra sticks with you, turning your meditation into a rhythmical release. It's a bit like mental chewing gum, keeping your mind masticating on a soothing phrase instead of gnawing on the day's worries.

In our modern hive of distractions, there's also Zen meditation, which is like the 'do not disturb' sign of spiritual practices. You just sit, let thoughts come and go, and probably have an epiphany or two about why avocados go bad so fast.

Of course, the minimalists might swoon over empty mind meditation. This is the 'less is more' approach—no mantras, no movements, just the sweet sound of nothingness. Make no mistake, it's less about an empty head and more about a full heart.

When life becomes a jazz improvisation that's gone sour, there's the harmony of qigong. A blend of meditation, breathing, and gentle movement, qigong is like the glue that can piece back together the pottery of your frazzled nerves.

Lastly, there's self-inquiry meditation. It's a journey inward where you get to play detective with your own existence. By examining the nature of the self, you might just find the plot twist in your personal narrative.

Remember, finding peace isn't a one-size-fits-all hat. Try on a few styles, mix and match, and soon enough, you'll find your meditative groove. Your inner peace is like a fingerprint—uniquely yours. So, take a deep breath and get cosy with these paths; your bliss-filled adventure awaits!

Chapter 4:
Conducting a Health Check

So you've dipped your toes into the blissful waters of breath control and meditation, and now you're ready to wade a little deeper, right? Consider this your personal pit stop, where you'll fine-tune that awesome vehicle of yours—your body. Let's take a moment, okay? A real, honest look under the hood to assess how the engine's running. This isn't about getting spooked by the occasional sputter or knock—everybody's got 'em. It's about becoming the best version of your grease monkey self, learning the ins and outs of what makes you tick.

We'll get all Sherlock Holmes on your physical wellbeing, without the magnifying glass, of course. And hey, we're not just talking carburettors and piston rings—your emotional and spiritual spark plugs need checking too. It's time to give your whole self a thorough once-over, balance those emotional chequebooks, and make sure your spirit's on track to hit that high-note harmony. Remember, no detail is too small when you're on the road toward feeling absolutely fabulous!

Body: The Physical Assessment

Alright, so let's switch gears and get physical – because this meat suit we walk around in, while it may come with a few stock parts, certainly needs regular tune-ups. Think of your body like the ultimate bio-machine that diligently gets us from point A to point B, and believe it or not, where it thrives most is in the care we gift it. So, let's dig our heels into the riveting world of physical assessments, shall we?

In the previous sections, we've been journeying through the mental and spiritual realms, tweaking our breathwork and marinating in the juicy practice of meditation. But now, it's time to check under the hood and examine the chassis – yep, I'm talking about your physical self. The body is no less critical in living your absolutely best life; it's the vessel that carries through every stellar moment.

Let's start with the foundation – posture. How's yours looking? Are you slouching like a moody teenager, or are you stacking those bones like a regal sovereign? Posture isn't just about looking poised — it's your body's alignment, and it impacts your energy, your breathing, your everything. So strut your stuff correctly, my friends, and your body will thank you.

The Blueprint for Bliss

Moving on, let's tap into the beat — your heart rate, that is. Knowing your resting heart rate can tell you a heck of a lot about your ticker's condition. It's a simple check you can do every morning before you roll out of bed. And hey, if it's consistently high, maybe it's time to consider that maybe those daily marathons of TV might need balancing out with, you know, an actual jog?

Next up, we have the food-fuel combo. What you put into this fantastic machine will forecast how well it runs. It's not rocket science — fresh, vibrant foods jazz up the system, while processed junk can gum it all up. Every bite is like choosing high-grade oil or sludgy leftovers for your engine — so maybe pick the avocado toast over the frosted cereal, at least most days.

Don't forget the hydration station. Odds are, if you're thirsty, you're already a bit dehydrated. Commit to guzzling H2O like it's your job because well, it kinda is. Dehydration is the nemesis of peak performance, so keep that water bottle as your trusty sidekick.

Here's a fun one — flexibility and balance. Stand on one leg, try touching your toes, shimmy into a yoga pose or two. These aren't just party tricks; they're telling of how limber and grounded your body is. These are also sly ways to assess if you're evenly keeled or possibly compensating for weaknesses. Ain't nothing wrong with finding out you're not a flamingo, but it's good to know where you stand.

Strength testing – now don't get intimidated. You don't need to be a bodybuilder, but a baseline of strength is like having a quality security system for your body. Push-ups, planks, squats – let's see what you've got! Remember, if it's challenging, it's changing you, and that's a good thing!

In order to maintain good physical health, it is essential to engage in regular exercise. But its benefits go far beyond the physical realm. Exercise also plays a vital role in aiding good mental health. When we exercise, our bodies release endorphins, which are natural chemicals that can help alleviate feelings of stress, anxiety, and depression. These chemicals also promote a sense of well-being and happiness, which can have a significant positive impact on our mental health.

Did you know that besides making you feel great, physical exercise can also uplift your self-esteem and confidence? Endorphins released during physical activity not only improve your mood but also give you a sense of accomplishment, which can lead to a more positive outlook on life.

When we set and achieve exercise-related goals, we feel a sense of accomplishment, which can translate into other areas of our lives. Exercise is also an excellent outlet for coping with stress, providing a sense of control over our lives, and helping to develop resilience.

While any type of physical activity can be advantageous, research suggests that aerobic exercise, such as running, cycling, or swimming, may be particularly effective at reducing symptoms of anxiety and depression. Strength training, such as lifting weights, can also be useful, as it can help to improve body image and self-esteem. Additionally, yoga and other mind-body exercises can help to lessen stress and anxiety while promoting a sense of calm and relaxation.

To achieve the best results, experts generally recommend getting at least 150 minutes of moderate-intensity exercise per week, spread out over several days. It's important to note that even engaging in small amounts of activity can be beneficial for one's mental health. Even if you don't have a lot of time or energy, incorporating a short walk or a few minutes of stretching into your day can make a big difference in how you feel emotionally and mentally.

Regular exercise is an excellent tool for maintaining good mental health. To conclude, it is essential to make exercise a part of our daily routine for overall well-being. By releasing endorphins, boosting self-esteem and confidence, and providing a healthy outlet for stress, exercise can assist us feel better both physically and mentally. Whether you prefer aerobic exercise, strength training, or mind-body exercises, finding a physical activity that you like, enjoy, and can stick with is key to reaping the benefits of exercise.

Let's not forget those pearly whites – yep, dental health. Your mouth is a gateway to the rest of your body. Good dental hygiene speaks volumes about your overall health. Grimace in the mirror if you need to, but check those gums and teeth regularly. A healthy smile can be a great indicator of a well-maintained machine.

Take notice of how you're hitting the hay – are you getting quality sleep? It's not just about the number of hours but how restorative those hours are. A physically well-maintained body will often reward you with sleep that's like a mini vacation each night. If you're tossing and turning, it's a red flag that needs attention.

Monitoring the numbers is key too — blood pressure, cholesterol, blood sugar – these aren't just figures your doc wags a finger at. They're crucial statistics in understanding the inner workings of your complex bio-machine. Take them seriously, but don't

The Blueprint for Bliss

let them scare you into paralysis. It's data – and data empowers change.

Your skin, oh the skin – it's your body's largest organ, so show it some love. Is it too dry, too oily, or just-right Goldilocks-style? Skin conditions can be a billboard for what's happening under the hood. Treat it well with hydration, and protect it from those sneaky UV rays.

Lastly, take note of your energy levels throughout the day. Are you running like an energizer bunny or dragging like a slug with a sunburn? Energy ebbs and flows, sure, but significant dips can hint at deficiencies or lifestyle imbalances. Listen to those signals — they're guiding you towards adjustments for better vitality.

In essence, your body is your temple, gym, and personal theme park all rolled into one – treat it with the respect and awe it deserves! Now, don't just sit there; stand up, stretch, bounce around a bit – let's get those physical vibes flowing. Conduct your physical assessment with joy and curiosity. Every discovery about how to optimise this beautiful biological masterpiece is a step closer to blissfulness.

So, let's wrap up this physical fanfare with a reminder that every bit of love you pour into this physical form radiates outwards. You're not just prepping yourself to look fab in a selfie, although that's a perk. You're gearing up for a life of zest, zeal, and zippy adventures. Now, onwards to the mind and spirit, where we'll take a deep dive into our emotional and spiritual assessments!

Mind and Spirit: The Emotional and Spiritual Assessment

So, you've just emerged from exploring the physical realm of your health check. Now, let's dive into the uncharted waters of your mind and spirit, shall we? Remember, your physical health might be on point, but if the mind and spirit aren't vibing right, it's like having a high-performance car with no gas. So, stick with me as we unpack the squishy stuff of feelings and the ethereal essence of the spirit.

First up, let's talk emotions – those slippery fish. Too often we treat our emotions like unwelcome house guests who overstayed their welcome. But guess what? They've got a permanent room in your brain's B&B. Instead of shunning them, let's get cosy and understand what they're here to tell us.

Now, an emotional assessment isn't your average checklist; it's not as straightforward as ticking off symptoms. It's about tuning in. How do you feel on an average day? Not just happy or sad, but the full spectrum – from jazzed about life to feeling like a deflated balloon. And hey, no judgment. If 'meh' is your baseline, that's our starting point, and that's okay.

Moving on to the spiritual side, don't get wigged out on me now. You don't need to be a yogi or a mystic to engage here. Spirituality is about what gives your life meaning. It doesn't have to be religious – it could be connecting with nature, jamming to your favourite music, or feeling part of something bigger than yourself. So, what lights your inner fire?

We can't talk emotions without bringing up our dear friend stress. Is stress your sidekick, always popping in to say hello, or is it like that distant relative you see once in a blue moon? Stress isn't inherently evil – it can be a motivator, but too much can turn your mind and spirit into a tangled mess.

Relationships:

Love and relationships play a critical role in shaping our lives. They can either fill our lives with joy and happiness or create a sense of emptiness and disappointment. The way we connect with others has a serious impact on our emotional and spiritual well-being. Therefore, it is crucial to take some time and assess our relationships, considering how they are influencing our lives positively or negatively. Are we surrounded by people who uplift and support us, or are we stuck in toxic relationships that drain our energy and leave us feeling unhappy?

By taking stock of our relationships, we can identify whether we are in a healthy balance or if we need to make changes to bring ourselves back into the green. It is essential to assess whether our relationships align with our values, goals, and aspirations. We must also consider whether we feel comfortable, respected, and valued in our relationships or if we feel emotionally drained, invalidated, or disrespected.

Therefore, it is crucial to take a deep breath and reflect on the people in our lives. Are they adding value to our lives, or are they causing us stress and discomfort? By gaining clarity on the quality of our relationships, we can make informed decisions about whether we need to make adjustments, set boundaries, or perhaps cut ties entirely. Remember, our relationships have the power to impact our lives significantly, so it's essential to prioritise healthy, supportive, and fulfilling relationships.

Objectivity, my friend, can be hard to come by when peering inward. Sometimes, what we think we feel isn't the full story – there's more under the hood. Hence, it's handy to have some feedback mechanisms. It could be a journal where you spill the beans, or maybe a trusty confidant who can give it to you straight.

Dealing with your emotions means not just recognising and naming them but understanding their origin story. Like why the long face when it rains or that warm fuzzy feeling when you help someone out. Your emotions are breadcrumbs leading you back to experiences that shaped you.

Alright, still with me? Good. Let's touch on your coping strategies. When life tosses you a hot potato, do you juggle or drop it? Reflect on the tools in your emotional toolkit – maybe it's time to sharpen some and chuck others. Sorry, retail therapy and binge-watching old sitcoms don't count as sustainable strategies.

Then there's the heart of the matter – your values and beliefs.

Our values and beliefs are the fundamental principles that govern our lives, shaping our thoughts, actions, and decisions. They act as our guiding stars, helping us navigate through the ups and downs of life. However, sometimes we may find ourselves feeling lost, uncertain, or disoriented, and that's when we need to take a step back and re-evaluate our values and beliefs.

By taking the time to reflect on our core principles, we can recalibrate our internal compass and set our sights on the true north that aligns with our spiritual GPS. This renewed sense of direction and purpose can help us stay true to ourselves and our beliefs, and make meaningful decisions that lead to a fulfilling life.

So, if you ever feel like something's off or you're not quite sure where you're headed, take a moment to check in with your values and beliefs. Doing so can help you realign with your true path and ensure that you're sailing toward true north as per your spiritual GPS. Remember, your values and beliefs are like your North Star - they will always guide you in the right direction if you listen to them.

Joy and Passion:

In life, it's important to not only focus on our responsibilities and obligations but also on the things that bring us joy and passion. These are the things that make us want to leap out of bed in the morning and dance in the kitchen. They are the experiences that light us up and fill us with a sense of purpose and fulfilment.

Taking the time to engage in activities that bring us joy and passion is essential for our emotional and spiritual wellness. It helps us to lower stress, improve mood, and feel more connected to ourselves and others. These experiences are like open tickets to the feel-good express and should be viewed as critical pit stops on the road to a fulfilling life.

So, whether it's painting, hiking, cooking, or anything else that brings you joy and passion, make sure you carve out time to do it regularly. It's not only good for your mental and emotional health but also for your overall well-being. Wait, can't forget about joy and passion. What makes you want to leap out of bed in the morning or dance in the kitchen? These are open tickets to the feel-good express and are critical pit stops on the road to emotional and spiritual wellness.

Forgiveness:

Have you ever experienced a situation where someone wronged you, and you found it difficult to forgive them? It's normal to have negative emotions in such situations, but holding onto grudges can become a burden. When we carry anger, resentment, or bitterness towards someone, it doesn't just affect them, but it also affects us. It's like we're carrying a backpack full of bricks, and it's exhausting.

Forgiveness is not about letting others off the hook, but it's also about freeing ourselves from the chains of negativity. It's about releasing ourselves from the emotional baggage that we've been carrying for too long. Forgiving doesn't mean forgetting, it doesn't mean that what happened was okay, and it doesn't mean that we have to reconcile with the person who hurt us. It simply means that we choose to let go of the negative emotions that are holding us back.

So, take a moment to reflect on your emotional backpack. Is there any emotional baggage that you've been carrying that could use some unpacking? Forgiveness can be difficult, but it's a vital step towards healing and moving forward.

Boundaries:

Setting boundaries can be a challenge, especially if you're usually saying yes to everything and everyone. However, it's important to remember that setting boundaries is not a selfish act; rather, it's an act of self-care and self-respect. It means being clear about your needs, values, and limits, and communicating them in a respectful and assertive way.

When setting boundaries, it's important to consider your physical, emotional, and mental well-being. For example, you may need to set boundaries around your work schedule to avoid burnout or around your social life to prioritise time with loved ones. You may also need to set boundaries around your personal space and time to ensure that you have time for self-reflection and self-care.

It's also important to remember that boundaries are not set in stone. As you grow and change, your boundaries may need to be adjusted. It's okay to reassess your boundaries and communicate them in a respectful and transparent way.

In summary, setting boundaries is an essential part of maintaining a healthy and balanced life. It allows you to guard your physical, emotional, and mental well-being, and to prioritise your needs and values in a respectful and assertive way.

Self Awareness:

Self-awareness is a crucial component of individuals' personal growth and development. It involves taking a closer look at your thoughts, feelings, and behaviours, and identifying patterns that may be holding you back from reaching your full potential. By identifying these patterns, you can understand their impact on your life and make positive changes to overcome them.

Being self-aware can assist you in recognising your strengths and weaknesses, and foster a deeper understanding of your values and beliefs. With this knowledge, you can better overcome life's challenges and achieve your goals with increased clarity and purpose. So, take some time to reflect on your inner world and get to know yourself better - your trusty lantern in the foggy realms of the mind and spirit will guide the way.

Gratitude:

Expressing gratitude can have a massive impact on our mental and emotional well-being. It's the practice of acknowledging and appreciating the good things in our lives, no matter how big or small they may be. Cultivating an attitude of gratitude can help shift our focus from what we lack to what we have. This change in how we view things can significantly impact our emotional state, mindset, and overall outlook on life.

When we take the time to count our blessings and express gratitude for them, we activate the pleasure centres in our brain, which release dopamine and other feel-good neurotransmitters. This can have an immediate impact on our mood and energy levels, helping us to feel more content, optimistic, and motivated.

So, what are some things that you can be thankful for? It could be something as simple as having a roof over your head, a warm meal, or good health. Or it could be something more personal, like a supportive family, loyal friends, or a fulfilling job. Whatever it is, try to focus on the positive aspects of your life and take a moment to express your gratitude for them.

The Blueprint for Bliss

You can create a mental list of things you're thankful for or even write them down. This practice of gratitude can help you cultivate a more positive mindset, reduce stress, and improve your overall well-being. So why not start today? Take a few minutes to reflect on the good things in your life, and watch your spirits perk up.

There it is, your whirlwind tour through the landscape of mind and spirit. Just remember, this isn't a one-and-done deal. It's a relationship with yourself that needs nurturing, like a garden or a sourdough starter. Keep at it, and watch your inner world bloom into a place that feels like home.

Chapter 5:
Nourishment for Happiness

Transitioning from checking your mental and physical batteries, now we're going to dive into the kind of fuel you're putting in your tank. Imagine happiness as a plant; you're not going to water it with lemonade and expect it to thrive, right? Instead, let's discuss how we can nourish that plant with the sort of sunshine and water that'll make it burst with life. It's about feeding your body things that make your mind say, 'Yeah, I can take on the world today!' And it's not just about chomping on kale and quinoa; it's about finding the foods that resonate with your body's unique chemistry and support your emotional well-being.

Think of food as a hug from the inside – we want to create a diet that feels like that really good, bear-hug kind of embrace. The goal? Crafting a diet that contributes to a mind so light, you could float through your day with a smile plastered on your face. Now that's what I call a blissful eating plan!

The Role of Diet in Emotional Well-being:

Hold onto your hats – well, actually, let's just gently place them beside us as we dive into the savoury world of eating your way to ecstatic moods. It turns out that what you put on your fork has the power to fiddle with your emotional fiddlesticks. Who knew? Spoiler alert: your gut did.

Diet isn't just about shaving inches off your waistline; it's, honest to goodness, a festival of chemical reactions that can bring your brain into the happy parade. Imagine serotonin and dopamine, the cheerleaders of your mood, getting their pompoms from the stuff you chew. Selecting foods rich in tryptophan, for example, isn't just a trivia fact; it's like sending a love letter to your brain saying, "Hey, let's make some good vibes, shall we?"

Now, let's talk gut feelings – they're a big deal. Your gut, that splendid tube of mystery, is so entwined with your emotions it could be Facebook official. The gut-brain axis is a gossip line where your digestive system and brain send each other status updates. And when your gut flora is living its best life, frolicking among fibre and nutritious eats, your mood is like a balloon on a sunny day – optimistically buoyant!

Here's a fun fact to snack on: inflammation isn't just a word that wins Scrabble; it's something that can crash the party in your brain. Certain foods, especially the kind processed within an inch of their lives, can cause inflammation, making your brain cells throw up their hands in despair. So, eating whole foods isn't just grand for your physique; it's like giving your neurons a spa day.

Feeling blue? Maybe you're not getting enough omega-3s. These smart little fatty acids are like the cool aunts and uncles of your mental health, soothing over rough patches and telling your stress hormones to take a hike. You'll find them lounging in the depths of cold-water fish, flaxseeds, and walnuts, ready to throw you a life jacket when you're swimming in turbulent emotional waters.

Don't forget the rainbow – and no, I'm not talking about chasing leprechauns. I mean plate up your veggies in all their colourful glory. Each pigment is nature's code for different micronutrients, which are like the Spice Girls of your body, working better together and bringing zest to your zest for life.

Who's got a sweet tooth? It's totally fine to crave a slice of cake, but remember, sugar is a smooth talker that doesn't follow through. It will take you on the highest of highs and then ghost you, leaving you in a slump. Moderation in treats is like setting curfews for your teenagers – it shows you care, and it prevents some seriously poor decision-making.

Eating regularly is not just a treat to your tastebuds; it's stability for your mood swings. When you keep your blood sugar steady, it's like giving your hormones a reliable heartbeat. Think of your meals as chill pills for your body's internal rhythm, keeping everything humming in sweet harmony.

Now, let's toast to hydration - cheers with your water bottles, folks! Water is the unsung hero in the orchestra of your moods. Dehydration is like a nagging critic in the front row, dampening the mood (ironically). Sipping the H2O keeps the brain in a fluid dance, nimble and quick.

A word on mindful eating – this isn't just for monks and health gurus. When you slow down and savour your meals, you're not just being fancy; you're allowing your brain to process the good vibes thoroughly. Chew with intention, and you might just taste the difference in your mood.

And before you think it's all kale and quinoa, relaxation is part of the diet too. Stress-eating isn't just a term for overindulging; it's a reminder that your emotions and mealtime choices do the tango together. So take a deep breath, meditate or do what gets you into your zen zone before raiding the kitchen. Eating stress-free is like jazz music for digestion – smooth and uplifting.

Kickstarting your day with a breakfast that includes protein is like sending your emotions first-class on a flight to Victory Ville. Protein gives you the staying power and keeps the hangries away – those growling stomach monsters that can make you snarly.

Treat spices like your spice of life – they can turn your meal from meh to magnificent. Not only do they pack flavour, but many spices, like turmeric, come with anti-inflammatory perks – because we love a good mood as much as we love a good curry, right?

An ensemble of vitamins and minerals are like the backup band for your brain, and they rarely miss a beat. Ensure you're getting enough B vitamins, magnesium, and vitamin D, because when you're well-stocked on these, your body sings in tune, and your mood is likely to follow. Plus, who wouldn't want the sunshine vitamin cheering them on?

Finally, let's chat about culinary creativity – it can be a balm to your soul. Trying new recipes and flavours keeps your taste buds and emotions intrigued. The kitchen becomes an experimental lab where serendipitous stews and heartfelt pies become part of your emotional vocabulary.

In sum, by flirting with fibres, romancing the rainbow of fruits and vegetables, embracing the essentials of hydration, and mastering the spice of life, we turn dining into a loving dialogue with our emotional well-being. Now, who's up for some mood-altering munchies?

Crafting Your Blissful Diet Plan

Is not about munching on kale while staring longingly at a doughnut. It's about creating a harmonious relationship with food that celebrates life, fuels your body, and uplifts your spirit. It's less about rigid restrictions and more about mindful choices that align with your journey to happiness.

Imagine your plate as a vivid palette, not just with colours but with flavours, textures, and nutrients. A blissful diet plan revolves around foods that not only tantalise your taste buds but also inject your body with vitality. We're talking fresh, whole foods that come loaded with the good stuff – think fibres, proteins, vitamins, and minerals.

Now I know what you're thinking, "But isn't eating healthy boring?" Let me tell you, it's as exciting as you make it! There's an abundance of fruits, veggies, grains, nuts, and legumes out there just waiting to dance on your palate. Each meal is an opportunity to experiment and discover combinations that you love.

Before we dive into the nuts and seeds of your blissful diet, let me remind you that guilty pleasures aren't off the table. Balance is key. If your soul sings for chocolate, let it serenade. The trick is to enjoy those treats in moderation and savour every bite. Work it into your plan rather than making it a forbidden fruit.

Think of your meals as a symphony, each one playing a different tune that resonates with your body's needs. A hearty breakfast might be a smoothie bowl topped with a medley of seeds and fruits. For lunch, perhaps a vibrant salad with a rainbow of veggies and a source of lean protein. Dinner might serenade with a whole grain melody, accompanied by a choir of spice-enriched lentils or roasted vegetables.

Hydration, although not always in the spotlight, deserves a standing ovation. Water is the conductor of your body's orchestra, orchestrating all sorts of cellular activities. Make it a practice to keep water by your side throughout the day. Infuse it with a twist of lemon, a sprig of mint, or a splash of fruit to keep things interesting.

Okay, enough with the symphony analogies, let's get practical. Start by crafting a weekly menu. It doesn't need to be worthy of a Michelin star; simplicity often sings the sweetest tunes. Planning ahead avoids

The Blueprint for Bliss

last-minute convenience-food temptations and keeps your diet in harmonious rhythm with your bliss goals.

Let's debunk the myth that healthy food takes an age to prepare. A blissful diet should blend with your lifestyle. Simple, swift recipes can be exceptionally nutritious and delicious. Have a go-to list of dishes that you can whip up in 30 minutes or less, perfect for those busy days when time is not on your side.

Consider the magic of meal prepping. Dedicating a couple of hours to prepare meals for the week can be a time-saving concerto. Cook in bulk, like grains and proteins, chop veggies, or portion out smoothie ingredients. Store them in the fridge, and you've got a backstage pass to quick, healthy meals on demand.

When you're on the go, don't let fast food throw you off. Keep healthy snacks stashed in your bag. Nut-and-fruit mixes, energy bars, or even a simple apple can be lifesavers when hunger strikes and you're miles from the convenience of your kitchen.

Eating out. Here's a tip: scan the menu for the hidden gems. Many restaurants offer wholesome, nutritious dishes; all you need to do is spot them among the less virtuous options. And hey, if you're feeling up to it, why not ask the chef for a tailored, bliss-appropriate dish? You may be pleasantly surprised by their willingness to make accommodations.

Having friends over? Turn it into a blissful feast! Home-hosted dinners don't have to be a threat to your diet plan. In fact, they're a golden opportunity to share your journey, flaunt those colourful dishes, and perhaps inspire your buddies to adopt their own blissful diet.

Tracking what you eat can be enlightening. No, it's not about being obsessive but rather about gaining insight into your eating patterns. It can help you tweak things here and there, ensuring you're on the right track toward dietary enlightenment. Just jot down or use one of those snazzy apps to document your culinary adventures.

Remember, the goal here is joy. Your meals should make you feel good both during and after eating. If certain foods leave you feeling weighed down or sluggish, they're probably derailing your bliss train. Listen to your body; it's the ultimate guru when it comes to your dietary needs.

In crafting your blissful diet, the overarching theme is to enjoy the journey – relish the flavours, delight in the preparation, and bask in the satisfaction that comes from treating your body like the temple it is. Let your meals be an expression of your intention to live a vibrantly happy life, and watch as every bite contributes to a more radiant you.

Chapter 6:
Enhancing Life Through Sleep

Just when you thought you had your daytime routine down to an invigorating science of breathwork, meditation, and superfoods, let's not forget the secret ingredient to a thriving existence — gloriously rejuvenating sleep. Think of your bed as a nightly spa for your brain, where neurons get pampered, memories are neatly filed away, and the mind-body connection gets polished until it shines. Dive into the zen-like rituals of sleep hygiene, and you'll be strategising rest like a chess master plotting their next winning move. Because let's face it, you're not just catching Z's, you're architecting dreams. And while we won't get into the nitty-gritty of REM cycles and power naps now (that's what this chapter's sub-sections are for), we'll transform your slumber into an art form that Michelangelo would envy if only he wasn't so busy painting ceilings. So fluff up your pillow, folks—the land of nod is about to become your nightly retreat that revamps your tomorrow.

Understanding Sleep Hygiene

So, you've been exploring the corners of your mind, tuning up your body, and infusing your spirit with all the good vibes. Kudos! But let me tell you, none of that will click into place if you're staggering around like a half-shut laptop, will it? Here's where 'sleep hygiene' struts onto the stage. It's not about having squeaky clean PJs or scrubbing behind your ears before bed – though, feel free if that floats your boat. No sir, it's all about habits, environments, rituals – essentially crafting the perfect symphony for slumber.

Sleep hygiene is akin to a cosy bedtime story for your nervous system. It's a series of recommendations meant to create a snooze-friendly environment, both in your bedroom and your head. It's more than just a routine; it's an art form. An art form that, when mastered, can have you kissing goodbye to those under-eye bags that not even a designer label can make look chic.

Now, if you're thinking you can keep scrolling through your endless feeds on social media until your eyelids are heavier than a week's worth of laundry, think again. Blue light from devices is like a double espresso for your brain. You might as well be turning cartwheels in your jammies if you're hitting the sheets post-screen spree. There's a fix for that – a sacred ritual called 'device detox' that, an hour before bed, can be a game changer. Trade your phone for a book, meditation, or contemplating your vast awesomeness. Your dreams will thank you.

Darwin may not have mentioned it, but a comfy mattress and pillows have climbed their way up the evolutionary ladder to become critical for survival, at least in the realm of quality z's. Your bed should be a cloud – a temple where stress fears to tread. So, start a pillow rebellion if you must. Just find what feels like a slice of nighttime nirvana to you.

Let's paint a little picture. Your room should be cooler than an A-list celebrity, and darker than their oversized sunglasses. So, while your mind is ready to dive into slumber, make sure your room is set to 'cave mode'. A cool, dark room simulates the natural drop in temperature and light that whispers to your brain, "Hey buddy, it's sleepy time."

Caffeine lovers, gather 'round and listen closely. Downing a cup of joe late in the day is like trying to lull yourself to sleep with a rock concert in your head. Caffeine has a half-life more stubborn than a toddler so let's cut it off past noon, shall we? Instead, sip on some herbal tea or warm milk and let the sandman do his thing.

Nap enthusiasts, I'm looking at you with a sympathetic squint. A midday siesta can be rejuvenating unless it's turning into a full-on hibernation session. Keep naps short and sweet, just like the best tweets, and early enough in the day that they don't throw a wrench in your nighttime ritual.

Dinner – that delicious prelude to the night. But let's skip the heavy, gut-busting meals close to bedtime. Indulge in that feast a bit earlier, and you'll be giving your body the green light to focus on getting you to dreamland rather than tackling the buffet you just offered it.

All right, so the clock's ticking, the yawns are multiplying, but there you are, letting the worries of the world play merry-go-round in your head. Let's break that cycle. Journaling or brain-dumping before bed can act like a sponge, soaking up all those buzzing thoughts so your mind can ease into tranquillity.

Let's not overlook the value of a consistent sleep schedule – and yes, that includes weekends. Try to tuck in and rise with the sun at the same time daily. Your internal clock will be more synchronised than the best boy bands of the '90s. That level of consistency? Absolutely dreamy.

And for the nights when sleep is playing hard to get, resist the urge to lie there, tossing like a salad. Get up, move to a different space, and engage in a calming activity. You want to associate your bed with successful snoozing, not a wrestling match with insomnia.

Speaking of wrestling, let's talk about exercise. We know it's like trying to decide which Netflix series to commit to – overwhelming at first, but so worth it. Regular activity can tire out your body just enough to make you love the sight of your pillow. However, try not to pump iron too close to bedtime unless you want your adrenaline doing the cha-cha when you're trying to hit the hay.

Now, alcohol might seem like a helpful sedative, but it's a sneaky one. Sure, it might send you off to the land of nod quicker, but you'll likely be bouncing back awake once its effects wear off. Aim for moderation and timing, and your REM cycle will groove uninterrupted.

For all the introspection and breathing exercises we do, our bedrooms can sometimes be cluttered with more than just clothes – I'm talking about the mental clutter too. Keep your sleeping environment minimalistic and peaceful. An oasis of calm in a world of chaos – that should be your bedroom's vibe.

Lastly, consider the power of a pre-sleep routine that gently nudicates you towards those sweet forty winks. What's a nudicate? It's that little nudge+education combo, something delightful like some light stretching, breathing exercises, or some good ol' fashioned reading (you know, from actual paper books).

In the grand symphony of life, sleep is the lullaby that keeps the rhythm balanced. Mastering sleep hygiene isn't just about tracking devices; it's an all-encompassing theme of creating harmony within your life – combining a dance of environmental tweaks and mental peace talks. Keep these tips in your dreamy toolkit, and you'll be snoozing your way to bliss in no time – with sleep hygiene as your new best friend!

Strategies for Restorative Sleep

So, you're tossing and turning, counting more sheep than there are in New Zealand, and still, sleep eludes you. Let me tell you, my friend, you're not alone in this midnight tango. But fear not! I've gathered some top-shelf strategies that will have you snoozing like a koala bear in no time. These are not your grandma's sleep tips - though, hats off to Granny for trying. So, let's dive into the luscious land of restorative sleep without another yawn. And remember, your bed is not a battleground - except on laundry day.

Firstly, listen to the rhythm of your own body clock. Are you a night owl who's trying to be an early bird? Stop right there. Tailoring your sleep schedule to fit your natural inclinations can be a revelation. It's like finding the right key for a lock. If life permits, shift your bedtime to when your body naturally feels sleepy. It's about working with your internal wiring, not against it.

Creating a sleep sanctuary is like setting the stage for a beautiful dreamy ballet. Your bedroom should be a temple dedicated to rest. This means: lights down low, keep it cool - not 'I'm stranded in the Arctic' cool, but about 19 degrees C of 'ahh, perfect.' Also, let's get the tech out of the boudoir. Seriously, your phone can sleep in the kitchen–it won't get lonely.

Ever heard of a bedtime routine? No, it's not just for toddlers. A winding-down ritual signals your body that it's time to shift into low gear. This might include a calming herbal tea instead of a late-night espresso shot, reading a book - preferably not a horror story - or some gentle stretching. It's about finding that sweet spot that whispers to your brain, "Hey buddy, it's sleepy time."

What about diet and sleep? They're like mac and cheese - they go together. Watching what you eat in the hours before bed can be game-changing. Avoid heavy, rich, or fiery foods that can cause an unwanted midnight spicy food festival in your stomach. Stick to lighter, easier-to-digest foods that soothe rather than rile up your digestive system.

Exercise is your friend. Well, most of the time. That love-hate relationship during a workout? It turns into pure love at bedtime. Regular physical activity helps deepen sleep. However, try not to turn into a nighttime warrior. Vigorous exercise too close to bedtime could leave you more hyped than a kid in a candy store. Timing is everything.

Naps are a double-edged sword. A short power nap can feel like a refreshing reboot, but snooze too long or too late in the day, and you might find yourself conducting a symphony of ceiling-staring at 2 AM. If you need that midday siesta, think of it as a catnap - not a bear hibernation session.

Mindfulness and relaxation techniques, oh my! From deep-breathing exercises to progressive muscle relaxation or even a little visualizing-your-happy-place action, these practices train your mind to transition from full-speed to serene. It's like teaching a hummingbird to glide gracefully instead of zipping like it drank a double espresso.

Let's talk about the darkness. No, not your teenage goth phase—we're talking literal darkness here. Melatonin, the sleep hormone, loves the dark. So consider blackout curtains, or for a budget-friendly option, a comfy sleep mask. It's not just a fashionable bedtime accessory; it's a ticket to Zzzzville.

Sound can play a significant role in your sleep experience. While you might not be able to control your neighbour's late-night bagpipe practice, you can introduce soothing sounds into your environment. White noise machines, a fan, or even a chill playlist can help mask pesky background noise. Think gentle ocean waves, not heavy metal drum solos.

If you're still rolling around, and you've tried everything above, let me introduce you to the paradoxical intention technique—fancy, right? It's a fancy term for trying to stay awake. Seriously, it reverse-psychologies your brain by removing the stress of trying to fall asleep. And when the pressure's off, your eyelids get heavier than a lead buffet.

Consider the humble journal as your sleep aid. Brain buzzing with thoughts? Put pen to paper. Jotting down worries or to-dos for the next day can clear your mind like a good spring cleaning. It's like telling your brain you've stored its concerns somewhere safe for the night. Pinky promise, you'll revisit them in the morning.

A gentle scent may help lead you into the Land of Nod. Aromatherapy isn't just for day spas. Essential oils like lavender aren't just pretty plants; they're the botanical buddies that help you relax. A drop or two on your pillow or diffused in the air can set the stage for slumberland.

Remember, consistency is key. Going to bed and waking up at the same time every day helps set your internal clock like a well-tuned watch. Sure, weekends might tempt you with a late-night Netflix binge or a sunrise social gathering, but try to keep your schedule like a comforting, familiar melody you can hum to.

Lastly, if all else fails and you find yourself wide-eyed, don't stay in bed growing increasingly frustrated. Get up, do something low-key and boring - think watching paint dry or grass growing - and when the drowsies kick in, then you head back to bed. Sometimes a little reset is all it takes.

There you have it, a treasure trove of strategies better than counting invisible farm animals. Play around with these tips and find the combo that hits the snooze-spot just right. And, as you drift off into a restorative sleep, remember that it's all about finding harmony in your habits. Sweet dreams are made of these - who am I to disagree?

Chapter 7:
Discovering Purpose

So you've eaten your greens, meditated like a Zen master, and you're getting more Z's than a beekeeper's buzzing buddies—what's next on this joyride to your best life? Enter Chapter 7: Discovering Purpose—the juicy part where your unique 'why' jolts you out of bed like a lightning bolt with espresso shot levels of zing. It's cool, we all get lost in life's supermarket sometimes, but it's about finding that special aisle that's got all the goods that spell YOU.

Purpose isn't just a fancy fable your grandma whispered about; it's the secret sauce to living a life that's as fulfilling as that last slice of pizza. It's about spotting the extraordinary in the oh-so-ordinary, crafting a life that mirrors the things that tickle your fancy and light fireworks in your heart. And don't worry, we're not talking about selling all your stuff and moving to a yurt (unless that's your jam)—it's about tuning into that inner voice that hums a tune only you can hear, and turning it up loud and proud. After all, when you're in sync with your purpose, every day's got that Friday feeling, even if it's just a mundane Monday morning! Let's roll up our sleeves and get those hands dirty in the garden of purpose, planting dreams and watching them bloom right where you are.

Finding Meaning in Everyday Life

We've all been there - standing in line at the coffee shop, zoning out during a daily commute, or slogging through the laundry and thinking, "Is this all there is?" Sure, we've talked about the grand designs of purpose and aligning your actions with your values. But here's the scoop: Discovering meaning isn't always about grand gestures; it's about the little moments, folks.

Consider the humble coffee bean. Alone, it's just a bean. But at the hand of a barista, it becomes a morning ritual, a source of warmth, a reason to smile. Can we uncover that same magic in the most mundane aspects of our lives? You bet your espresso shot we can!

You see, life's about perspective. The routines that feel tiresome are often opportunities dressed in work clothes. The trick lies in tweaking our lens to spot the marvellous in the monotonous. A commute becomes time to reflect, to learn through podcasts or audiobooks, or to marvel at the web of human lives intersecting your own.

The Blueprint for Bliss

Then there's nature's free show - ever watched the sun play peek-a-boo behind skyscrapers? Simple, sure, but striking if you're tuned in. Observing the rhythm of the day, noting the ebb and flow, brings a profound connection to the cosmos. It's in these moments that our everyday lives become canvases for meaning.

Let's not overlook connections either. Each person you encounter, from the bus driver to the mail carrier, carries a galaxy of stories. Engaging with others, even briefly, can turn an ordinary exchange into a memorable encounter. It's humanity in high definition, and you're part of it.

So, about that laundry – think of it as a Zen garden. Might sound funny, but stick with me. Folding shirts becomes a meditation, a way to practice mindfulness, and a moment to express gratitude for the hands that wove the fabric. Getting playful with perspective injects joy into what's dull, don't you think?

Work, ah yes, the daily grind. But isn't it also the chance to craft something unique, to solve puzzles, to connect and create? When we shift from seeing "just a job" to exploring our tasks as avenues for growth and ingenuity, even Monday has the potential to sparkle.

And hey, let's dish about meals. They're not just about eating; they're culinary journeys, chances to share stories with loved ones, or to savour the art of spices and flavours. Even if it's just a sandwich, taste it like it's a chef's masterpiece – because today, it's your masterpiece.

Those habits you're forming? Whether it's drinking more water or stretching in the morning – they're not just to-dos. They're acts of reverence for the incredible machine that is your body, a toast to your health, and a pat on the back from you to you.

And let's not forget challenges. Those obstacles that pop up, they're not just roadblocks; they're your personal trainers in disguise, bulking up your resilience and flexing your problem-solving muscles. Bring it on, life – we're ready for our workout!

Ever thought about the art of conversation? Each dialogue is a dance, a chess game of words, a chance to learn and laugh. Let's treasure the pauses, the quips, the shared glances – in these beats, we find the richness of relationships.

Now, consider your hobbies. It's not about killing time; it's about living time. Whether you knit, run, read, or game – these aren't trivial pursuits; they're threads in the tapestry of your unique existence. Masterpieces take time, and your life is a work of art in progress.

Sure, life's routine can feel like a loop, but every loop is a chance to jump higher, to be bolder, to learn a new joke, or to spot a different shade of green on your walk. When you embrace each day as a treasure hunt, X marks the spot on your calendar.

And as night settles in, don't just plop into bed. Reflect on the day's gifts, the moments of connection, of beauty, of accomplishment. Today was one of a kind, and you were the chief architect of its meaning.

So, what's the takeaway? Meaning isn't handed to us – it's crafted by us, in the tiny bits of extraordinary we weave into the ordinary. And remember, the present is called a gift for a reason. Unwrap today with the excitement of a child on their birthday, and delight in the mundane majesty of it all. After all, you're living your best life one uniquely ordinary day at a time.

Designing a Life Aligned with Your Values

Think about a ship on the vast ocean without a compass. That kind of meandering is fine for a relaxed Sunday sail, but when you're determined to reach a destination, just bobbing on the waves won't cut it. Your values are like a compass - they point you to your true north. So, let's chat about how tailoring your life around your values is like crafting an epic voyage across your personal sea of dreams.

First off, identifying your values is similar to drawing out your personal treasure map. You wouldn't set sail without knowing where X marks the spot, right? Jot down what matters most to you. We're talking about those non-negotiables, the things that, when someone steps on them, it's like they've pushed the big red button marked 'Do Not Push.' Maybe it's family, honesty, or maybe even spontaneity - whatever floats your boat.

Next, you're gonna want to inspect your current life's blueprint - yes, the one you're living right now. Are there any leaks? Any creaky boards that don't resonate with your values? This isn't about guilt-tripping yourself because you haven't been living like a saint. It's about getting real about where you're at and where your compass is actually pointing.

When you understand what your values are, you're going to see the gaps clearer than ever. Ever tried fitting a square peg in a round hole? Spoiler alert: It doesn't work. When your life doesn't align, it feels just like trying to force that square peg into place. So, it's renovation time - time to patch up the misalignments and make room for more of what truly counts to you.

Let's take action, implement those values like you're planting a garden. You wouldn't just throw those seeds willy-nilly and hope for the best. No, you place them intentionally, give them the love, sunlight, and water they need to blossom. Every choice you make - how you work, play, and live - should plant more of these values into the soil of your life.

Here comes a curveball, though - sometimes what we say we value and what we actually spend our time and energy on are two different things. If you say you value health, but you've got a 'reserved' sign on the couch and a romantic relationship with your snack drawer, it's time to reexamine. Again, it's not about rocking a guilt trip; it's about aligning your actions with your compass.

Making decisions based on your values isn't just some philosophical hokey-pokey; it's the nuts and bolts of a fulfilling life. When faced with choices, big or small, ask yourself which option is more aboard the values express. Trust me, making choices will feel less like a shot in the dark and more like a strategic move on your master plan.

And when it comes to setting goals, align them with your value compass, too. Chasing after someone else's treasure won't bring you a sliver of joy if it's not what you truly cherish. Set goals that make your heart sing louder than your shower performances. That's when you know you're on the right track.

But remember, designing a life aligned with your values isn't about perfection. It's like yoga - it's a practice. Some days you're the warrior pose, and other days you're the "I need a five-minute savasana" pose. The point is to keep at it, to keep steering the ship in the direction of your true north.

Now, be prepared to bid adieu to things that don't align with your values - that job that's crushing your soul or that habit that keeps poking holes in your self-esteem. It might feel like you're losing a part of your life, but you're actually shedding the excess weight to sail faster towards your utopia.

As you do this, you're going to feel the waves. Some people might not get it, and that's okay. The point isn't to win a popularity contest; it's about staying true to yourself. Hold fast to your compass, and let others sail their own seas.

But wait, there's more to this than just solo sailing. Share your values with your crew - your friends, family, and colleagues. When they know what matters to you, they can help keep you on course. They can be your lighthouse in the fog, the Polaris in your night sky.

Don't forget to celebrate the milestones too. When you live by your values, every step forward deserves some confetti and a high-five, even if it's just a mental one. Pause, appreciate the view, and then set sail again.

Finally, reevaluate your values from time to time. Life's about change, and it's natural for your values to evolve. What mattered a decade ago might be taking a back seat now, and that's okay. Update your treasure map, polish your compass, and keep your sails adjusted to the winds of life.

In conclusion, designing a life aligned with your values isn't just about grand gestures and monumental shifts. It can be, but it's also in the little things - the choices you make day in, day out. These steps create a tapestry of a life well-lived, a life that's authentically yours. Let your values lead the way, and you'll be surprised at the richness of the journey. Your happiness, your best life, is not at some distant shore - it's in the sailing itself.

Chapter 8:
Rewiring Subconscious Beliefs

Ever felt like your own mind is plotting a sneaky sabotage festival behind your back—complete with streamers, party hats, and limiting beliefs doing the limbo under your hopes and dreams? Well, it's time to crash the party and rewire those pesky subconscious beliefs that are holding you back. The maze inside your noggin' is filled with pathways forged during slap-your-forehead moments, and well-meaning but misguided lessons learned from your bowl-cut days. But guess what? With a sprinkle of awareness and a dash of determination, you can transform those pathways into superhighways that lead straight to your best life. It's like hacking into your own brain and installing the coolest, most empowering update yet.

Get ready to become a beliefs electrician, because you're about to find those short circuits and flip the switches that illuminate your potential. Let's deep dive into mind makeover mode and tweak the wiring beneath that fabulous hairdo of yours. And by the end, not only will you be the proud owner of a brand spanking new mindset, but you'll also have the know-how to keep that mental motherboard running like a dream.

Identifying Self-Sabotage and Limiting Beliefs

It's like we're all born with a mental toolkit. Unfortunately, it often comes packed with a bunch of faulty gadgets called limiting beliefs and self-sabotage mechanisms that nobody remembers ordering. These dodgy devices can really hamper your chances of living your best life. But here's the good news: You've got the power to identify and toss them out for good. Let's dive in and declutter that mental space!

Now, self-sabotage is your own psychological thriller in real-time. It's you, stealthily undermining your own goals and dreams. You might think, "Why would I do that?" Well, it's like there's a secret agent in your brain that thinks keeping things 'safe' and status quo is the mission at all costs. Your job is to catch that sneaky operative in the act!

Think about a time you almost got what you wanted but then, somehow, "accidentally" torpedoed it. Maybe you procrastinated on preparing for a big presentation or started a silly argument right when a relationship was getting good. These are telltale signs that your inner saboteur is on the loose.

Let's shine a light on some common limiting beliefs, too. These puppies are the myths that you've accepted about yourself over time - like "I'm not good enough," "I can't succeed," or "Happiness is for others, not me." If your belief system were a garden, these would be the weeds, and it's high time you pulled them out.

Detecting these beliefs requires a bit of self-reflection. You've got to play detective and trace back your actions (or inactions) to the thoughts that sparked them. Why didn't you ask for that deserved raise? Is there a sneaky suspicion in your mind that believes you're not actually worth it? Bingo, you've spotted a limit!

To really get to the root, think about the narrative you tell yourself when you're all alone. The things you say to yourself when nobody's watching can be telling. Are you your own hype-man or your own worst critic? If you're constantly picking at your confidence like it's a batch of day-old fries, there's work to do.

But how did these self-sabotaging rascals and beliefs get into your toolkit in the first place? Well, they're often relics from past experiences - like the hand-me-downs you got from family or friends that never really fit right. You might have learned to doubt yourself early in life, or maybe a failure became a bit too defining. The past can be sticky, but remember, it doesn't have the final say. You do.

A crucial part of beating self-sabotage is setting your environment up for success. It's like if you wanted to avoid eating junk food, you wouldn't camp out in a doughnut shop, right? Similarly, if you surround yourself with negativity or high-stress situations, your inner saboteur gets way too comfy. So, audit your surroundings. Are they supporting your growth or feeding your fears?

Sometimes acknowledging these unhelpful patterns can feel like opening Pandora's box, but it's more like cleaning out your attic. It might be dusty and full of cobwebs, but once it's clean, you realise how much valuable space you've got up there. Techniques for transformation are your dusters and broomsticks, ready to clear the mess.

After you've scoped out the landscape of your limiting beliefs, it's time to challenge them. Ask yourself: "Is this belief an absolute truth or an opinion dressed up as fact?" Get used to demanding evidence from these restrictive thoughts, and you'll often find they're about as factual as a tabloid headline.

Reshaping these beliefs is like sculpting with clay; it takes time and endurance. Begin by moulding small, positive affirmations about yourself. If your limiting belief is "I'm not a successful person," start sculpting the counter-belief "I am capable of success" with daily reminders and examples of your past wins, however small they may seem.

Action is the nemesis of self-sabotage. It's hard to undermine your dreams while you're busy making them come true. So, make commitments that counteract the sabotage. If you fear public speaking, sign up for a workshop. If you dread failure, commit to a new project. Action builds the resilience that self-sabotage dislikes.

Don't underestimate the power of support systems either. We often keep our self-doubts and sabotage habits a secret, but sharing them with trusted pals can be the breakthrough. Friends can peel back the layers of your limiting beliefs with you, offering the fresh perspective of an outsider looking in.

By identifying these gremlins in your mentality, you're taking the first steps not just toward managing them but toward a full-blown victory dance of self-improvement. Keep at it, and you'll find these challenges are just the pre-game warmup to the main event—living that blissful life you're after.

As you close this chapter, remember that the battle against self-sabotage and limiting beliefs is won through awareness and perseverance. By paying close attention to your thought patterns and continuously challenging them, you'll not only set yourself free from these constraints, you'll also pave a clear path towards your personal bliss. So let's roll up those sleeves and get to mental decluttering—the best version of you is waiting on the other side!

Techniques for Transformative Change

Now, we've come a long way from identifying those crafty little subconscious beliefs that like to play hide and seek in the darkest corners of our minds. But shining a flashlight on them is one thing; teaching them to dance to a new tune is another game altogether. So, let's dive into some transformative techniques that'll make those beliefs boogie in a way that benefits our lives and our happiness.

First things first, let's chat about the art of mindfulness. Yes, I know, mindfulness is like that one health nut friend who won't shut up about kale smoothies. But bear with me - this stuff is potent. Practising mindfulness helps you become the observer of your thoughts, not the doormat. When you notice a limiting belief tiptoeing across your brain, you can acknowledge it, nod politely, and then send it on its way without an invitation to return.

Next on our list is the juicy technique of visualisation. Imagine it's not just for Olympic athletes or those wanting to manifest a parking spot. If you can picture your life without those persistent limiting beliefs, you've already put one foot on the path to change. See yourself crushing goals, embracing happiness, and tossing those old beliefs out like last year's fashion faux pas. Feels good, doesn't it?

Let's keep the momentum going with some good ol' affirmations. Now, I'm not talking about gazing into a mirror and whispering sweet nothings to yourself - unless that's your jam. Affirmations are like setting a GPS for where you want your beliefs to go. Speak them, write them, sing them in the shower - whatever it takes to drill in those positive truths.

But wait, there's more - journaling! It's not just for teenage angst. Writing down your thoughts, feelings, and those sneaky subconscious beliefs gives you a powerful overview of your mental landscape. Better yet, tracking your progress through journaling is like giving yourself a high-five for every step forward.

Okay, brace yourself for some tough love with shadow work. It's all about embracing every part of you, including the bits you'd rather not RSVP. Getting cosy with your shadow self helps transform those darker parts into strength and wisdom. No more shoving them under the rug—let's put them to work instead.

Shadow work is a process of self-discovery that involves acknowledging and accepting all aspects of ourselves, even the ones that we may not be proud of or comfortable with. It can be challenging but incredibly rewarding because it helps us transform our weaknesses and fears into strengths and wisdom.

By embracing our shadow self, we can unlock our full potential and become more self-aware, compassionate, and empathetic individuals. Instead of suppressing or denying our shadow self, we can learn to work with it and use it to our advantage.

This process requires us to confront our deepest fears, insecurities, and vulnerabilities. It involves a willingness to be honest with ourselves and to take responsibility for our actions and behaviours. But by facing our shadows head-on, we can gain a greater understanding of ourselves and our place in the world.

So, if you're ready to embark on a journey of self-discovery and growth, embrace your shadow self and let's put those darker parts of you to work. Remember, it's not about being perfect, it's about being human and embracing all that comes with it.

Cognitive-behavioural techniques can also be superheroes in disguise when it comes to transformative change. By challenging and replacing distorted thoughts with more balanced ones, you're essentially giving your brain a new set of lenses—minus the limiting belief smudges.

Moving the body is another secret weapon. Dance, jog, or simply stroll around the block—physical movement shakes up the old energy and welcomes the new. Ever heard of 'embodied cognition'? Yeah, your body and mind are in cahoots, and when one moves, the other grooves.

Coaching:

Let's not forget about the role of mentors and coaches. Sometimes, a guiding hand or a fresh perspective can catapult you through transformation faster than you can say "quantum leap".

Having a mentor or coach in your personal or professional life can be incredibly beneficial. These individuals have more experience and knowledge in a particular area and can offer guidance, support, and advice on how to improve and achieve your goals. They can provide unique perspectives and fresh ideas you may not have considered.

Think of a mentor or coach as a Yoda to your Luke Skywalker. Just as Yoda helped Luke harness the Force and become a Jedi. Having a mentor or coach can be incredibly helpful in unleashing your full potential and achieving success. They can offer insights and strategies that can catapult you through transformation faster than you can imagine - just like a quantum leap.

So, if you're feeling stuck or uncertain about your next steps, it may be beneficial for you to consider seeking a mentor or coach who can provide guidance and support as you navigate your journey. With their support and expertise, you have the potential to accomplish great things and reach new heights in both your personal and professional life.

Support:

Having a solid support system is equally crucial. Surround yourself with people who water the flowers, not the weeds, in your garden. They're the cheerleaders, the tough-lovers, the ones who see the phoenix within you, even when you feel like a pile of ashes.

When we talk about achieving our goals and fulfilling our dreams, it's easy to focus solely on our own efforts and forget the importance of having a supportive community around us. But the truth is that having a solid support system is equally crucial to our success.

The people we surround ourselves with can have a significant impact on our mindset, our motivation, and our overall outlook on life. That's why it's so important to choose our friends and associates carefully, making sure that we are surrounding ourselves with people who will lift us up and encourage us to be our best selves.

In this context, the metaphor of the garden is especially apt. Our lives are like gardens, and the people we surround ourselves with are like the gardeners. The best gardeners are the ones who know how to nurture and care for the plants that they want to grow, while weeding out the ones that are harmful or don't belong. In the same way, the best friends and supporters are the ones who "water the flowers" in our lives, helping us to grow and thrive, while avoiding the "weeds" that can hold us back or drag us down.

When we have a supportive community around us, we are better equipped to face the challenges and setbacks that life tends to throws our way. We have cheerleaders who will celebrate our successes and help us to keep going when we feel discouraged. We have tough-lovers who will hold us accountable and challenge us to be our best selves. And we have people who can see the potential within us, even when we can't see it ourselves.

So, if you're working towards a goal or trying to make a change in your life, remember the value of having a supportive community around you. Surround yourself with people who will help you to "water the flowers" in your life, and avoid those who will "weed" your garden. With the right support, you can overcome any obstacle and achieve your dreams.

And who could dismiss the power of humour?

Humour is a powerful tool that we can use to our advantage in many different situations. Laughing in the face of adversity can help us to take the sting out of a difficult situation, and to find a way to move forward despite the challenges we are encountering. Similarly, when we laugh at the ridiculousness of old beliefs that no longer serve us, we are able to diminish their power over us and to embrace new, more empowering ways of thinking.

One of the reasons why humour is so powerful is that it brings lightness to situations that might otherwise feel heavy and overwhelming. When we are weighed down by negative or unwanted subconscious beliefs, it can feel as though we are carrying a heavy burden. But by introducing laughter and humour into the mix, we can create a sense of lightness that helps us to feel more optimistic and hopeful about the future.

In short, humour is a valuable tool that we can use to help us navigate through life's challenges. Whether we are facing a difficult situation or trying to let go of old beliefs that no longer serve us, humour can be a powerful ally that helps us to stay positive, optimistic, and focused on our goals. So the next time life throws you a curveball, try to find the humour in the situation - you might be surprised at just how much it can help!

Now let's talk about setting intentions—because nothing says "I'm serious about change" like a good old-fashioned intention. It's like making a pinky promise with the universe, and it's got some severe mojo for propelling you in the right direction.

Lastly, celebrate every win, no matter how small.

Celebrating your progress is an essential part of any journey towards self-improvement. It helps you to appreciate the small victories along the way, no matter how insignificant they may seem. For instance, suppose you find yourself stuck in a cycle of negative thoughts and manage to catch yourself midstream and flip the switch to a more positive outlook. In that case, that's a significant achievement that deserves recognition and celebration.

By celebrating these moments, you create a sense of momentum that propels you forward towards bigger and better things. It's like fuel for your motivation engine that keeps you going even when the going gets tough. So, make sure you take the time to pat yourself on the back and celebrate every win, no matter how small. It makes all the difference in the world.

The Blueprint for Bliss

Implementing these techniques isn't a one-and-done deal. It's an ongoing groove-a-thon with your subconscious mind. Keep at it, and those limiting beliefs will start to look like outdated wallpaper—ready to be peeled off for good.

So, while we wrap up this jam session on transformative techniques, remember that change is as much about the journey as it is the destination. Keep tinkering, keep playing, and keep transforming. The blissful life you're crafting isn't just a possibility—it's your new reality in the making.

And with that, we march on to the next chapter, where we'll tie all these threads together, creating a tapestry that's vibrant with integrated body, mind, and spirit. Stay tuned because it only gets better from here!

Chapter 9:
Integrating Body, Mind, and Spirit

So, we've danced through the early stages of setting the stage for a blissful life, from controlling our breath to rewiring our deepest subconscious beliefs, and now it's time to bring it all together. Integrating body, mind, and spirit isn't just some fancy talk that sounds good on paper; it's the true essence of harmony. Imagine your physical, mental, and spiritual selves blending like a smoothie that's just the right flavour for your soul. It's like being the maestro of your own personal orchestra - every facet of you tunes up and plays in the most captivating symphony.

Don't just take care of your body and call it a day, or meditate and think you've hit enlightenment. Nah, we're going for the gold medal in personal synergy. It's about crafting those habits that ensure your whole being is high-fiving each other, from the cells in your toes to the thoughts soaring through your noggin to that sparkling spirit of yours. Easy? Not always. Worth it? You bet your kale smoothie it is!

Holistic Approaches for Balance

Let's dive right into the heart of holistic harmony. Imagine your life as a symphony. Each instrument—your body, mind, and spirit—plays a critical part in the grand performance. If one instrument is off, the entire piece is out of whack, right? That's where holistic approaches swoop in to save the day, tuning each part to perfection so the music of your existence plays smoothly.

We're not just talking about popping a vitamin and calling it a day. Nope. We're looking at an all-encompassing, full-circle, give-it-everything-you've-got kind of balance. You've got to think of yourself as a puzzle where each piece is essential: good nutrition, solid relationships, meaningful work, and positive thoughts. Now, let's connect those puzzle pieces without losing any under the couch!

First up, let's talk body talk. No, not that '80s hit song, but the way your body communicates its needs. Listening to your body is like tuning into your favourite radio station—you get the best tracks when the signal is strong. So, tune into what this temple is telling you! A stretch here, a rest there. It's all about honouring the requests of your flesh and bones.

Swinging to the other side, we have the mind. Ever have so many tabs open in your brain that you can practically hear the dial-up internet sound? Let's close some of those tabs by learning to filter the info inflow. Just like you declutter your closet, declutter your mind. Focus on what serves you and discard the rest.

And then, there's the enigma, the spirit. This is where things get a bit mystical, but stick with me. Spirit is the breath of life in your actions, the love in your laughter, the peace in your pause. Feeling connected to something greater can give your daily hustle a whole new rhythm.

So how do we get this trio to dance in sync? Through intentional practices. Meditation? Absolutely. A sprinkle of yoga? Yes, please. And don't forget about spending time in nature. Let the whisper of the wind and the chorus of the birds be your grounding playlist.

Did someone say eating greens? Well, maybe not out loud, but your gut probably whispered it. Fruits, veggies, grains—they're the unsung heroes in our quest for balance. Imagine them as the backup dancers to your lead singer, quietly enhancing the performance of your life.

But let's not neglect those sweet zzz's. Sleep isn't just for the dead (or the babies). It's for the living, the thriving, the go-getters who understand that rest is the secret sauce to a balanced life. Think of it as recharging your batteries so you can light up the world with your energy.

Now, embrace the power of connection. Call an old friend, hug your pet, share a smile with a stranger. These connections tether us to the world and add weight to our existence. They are the strings that, when woven together, create the safety net that catches us when we falter.

Are you keeping up with your journal? Yes, that's a holistic tool too! Jotting down thoughts, dreams, and even that weird thing your neighbour did last Tuesday is all part of understanding the full picture of your life.

Don't be that person who rushes through showers just as a necessity. Make it a sensory experience! Light a candle, play some tunes, and let the water wash away more than just physical dirt. Shower thoughts can be revolutionary; just ask any philosopher or shampoo bottle reader!

Breathwork isn't just for the yoga mat, friends. Those deep breaths can be taken anywhere: in line at the grocery store, during a tricky work meeting, or while listening to Aunt Marge's vacation stories for the umpteenth time. Just breathe and balance.

Imagine your thoughts as a garden. You've got to weed out the negatives to let the positives bloom. Mindfulness is about becoming the gardener of your internal landscape, carefully choosing what you plant and nurture in the fertile soil of your mind.

And let's not forget about the arts. Painting, writing, singing, dancing—these aren't just hobbies; they're the expressions of your soul. Engage in them, and watch how they colour your inner and outer worlds with vibrancy.

Lastly, laugh. Laugh until your belly aches and tears stream down your cheeks. Humour is not just medicine; it's the elixir for a balanced life. Don't take it all so seriously. After all, isn't life just one grand, cosmic joke with excellent timing?

By now, you're likely seeing how everything interconnects, how the balance comes from the symphony of actions, thoughts, and emotions. It's not about being perfect—it's about being harmoniously imperfect. So go ahead, try a little bit of everything. Stir it up. Create your own holistic cocktail for life's grand feast. And remember, even when you wobble, you're still on the path, you're still part of the music. That, my friend, is balance.

So, as we string our bow and set our arrow towards the bullseye called "best life," remember that holism is about targeting every ring on that target. It's in the trying, the mixing, and the harmonising that we find our own unique balance. Keep this symphony playing, my melodious friend, and watch your life compose itself into a masterpiece of bliss.

Creating Synergy for Optimal Living

Now there's a phrase that could scare the pants off any self-respecting couch potato. But let's not get too hung up on formalities. What we're really talking about here is shaking hands with your body, mind, and spirit, and getting them to play nice together in the sandbox of life. It's about becoming the ultimate teammate to yourself, and who wouldn't want to high-five their way through life?

Consider for a moment a trio of musicians. If they're not in sync, the result is a cacophony that makes your ears beg for mercy. But when they find their rhythm? Ah, pure harmony. That's what creating synergy in your life is about. It's finding your rhythm, across all aspects of your being, to live a life that sings to you - and maybe even inspires a little toe-tapping in others.

First things first: let's get our head in the game. This isn't just about the kale you put in your smoothie or the number of sun salutations you do before breakfast (though, hey, not knocking those). It's about feeding your head with thoughts that elevate, not negate. Your mind's garden, and while no garden is without weeds, it's up to you to make sure the greens outnumber the meanies. Reading uplifting material, indulging in constructive conversations, and practising mindfulness can keep your mental soil fertile for positivity.

And your body? It's not just a temple - it's a rockin' dance floor. It craves movement like your brain craves a good joke. So why not give it what it wants? Whether it's shaking your booty in a Zumba class, playing footsie with nature on a hike, or testing the waters with some stand-up paddleboarding, find that physical activity that makes you feel alive. Because when your body feels good, you're halfway to heaven.

Now, let's talk about the often-overlooked spirit - no, not the one in the bottle - your inner spirit. It's that little spark inside that lights up when you're doing what you love, or when you're in the presence of those who make your heart do cartwheels. Nurturing your spirit might look like carving out time for creative hobbies, volunteering for causes you're passionate about, or simply practising daily acts of kindness. A nurtured spirit is like a glowstick at a rave - it can't help but brighten up the place.

So, how do we get these three - body, mind, and spirit - to tango together? One word: intention. It's the GPS system for your life. When you live with intention, each decision and action is a step on the dance floor of your chosen path. It might not be an easy waltz, more like a thrilling salsa that keeps you on your toes, but that's where the fun lies, isn't it?

Balance doesn't always come naturally, but it's attainable with a little practice. Think of it as riding a bike - you might wobble a bit at first, but soon you're cruising with the breeze in your hair. Start small with integrating practices from each area of life. A morning might include affirmations (mind), a brisk walk (body), and meditation (spirit). You're not just multitasking; you're multithriving!

Remember, communication is key, and not just the kind you do with emojis. Listen to your body when it whispers for rest, to your mind when it screams for quiet, and to your spirit when it sings for joy. Acknowledging these communications ensures you're on the winning team of yourself.

And as you find synergy, remember, consistency is your best buddy. It's not about making one grand gesture to your well-being; it's the little daily high-fives you give yourself that add up to a standing ovation over time. Small, consistent synergistic actions are the stepping stones to a river of well-being that flows toward optimal living.

Let's not forget the power of flexibility—I'm not just talking about touching your toes. Life will throw curveballs, fastballs, and the occasional knuckleball. Being flexible in your approach to creating synergy means you can adapt and keep playing the game, even when the rules change without warning.

When we think of synergy, we often think of strength, but let's not underestimate the power of rest. Even the Sun takes a break, dipping below the horizon to let the stars have their time to shine. Rest is the unsung hero of synergy, providing your body, mind, and spirit the space to rejuvenate and come back stronger. Honour your need for downtime as much as your urge to climb mountains.

As you journey through this quest for optimal living, sprinkle in a healthy dose of humour. Let's face it, life is downright hilarious sometimes, and laughing at the absurdities can be the best medicine. Plus, a good guffaw does wonders for your abs—talk about a two-for-one deal!

In the grand tapestry that is your life, think of synergy as the thread that weaves through each day, connecting the moments, the experiences, and the lessons. It's the colour that pops, the pattern that pleases, the texture that tantalises. With each stitch, you're creating a masterpiece that is uniquely yours.

And if you stumble along the way, if the synergy seems to slip through your fingers like sand, remember,

The Blueprint for Bliss

it's all part of the process. Even a well-oiled machine needs a tune-up now and then. It's not about perfection; it's about progress, about the dance. And boy, what a dance it is when you have body, mind, and spirit moving in lockstep to the beat of your own drum.

So as we wrap up this little pow-wow on synergy, take a moment to appreciate the magic that happens when you align different facets of your life. It's like watching the pieces of a puzzle click into place, revealing a picture so beautiful, it makes you wonder why you didn't start piecing it together sooner. With each step toward creating that synergy, you're one step closer to living your best life—the life that's been waiting for you to take the lead and sashay into your greatest potential.

Now, go ahead, set the world on fire with your synchronicity. May you find your rhythm, your harmony, and a bounty of high-fives along the way. Here's to creating synergy for optimal living, to not just surviving, but thriving in the melodic medley of life's grand symphony.

Chapter 10:
Cultivating Self Love

Imagine gazing into a mirror with the kind of adoration usually reserved for hot fudge sundaes - that's where we're headed in this chapter. Having untangled the knots of limiting beliefs and learned to moonwalk across the mind-body-spirit dancefloor, it's time to turn up the self-love anthems and be your own hype person. You're not just going to like yourself, you're going to be absolutely smitten, because self-love isn't just about accepting compliments without a sarcastic retort; it's about embracing every quirk, celebrating each triumph, and offering kindness to yourself on the rough days. Let's ditch the inner critic for a cheerleader that's going to root for you harder than a soccer mom with a caffeine buzz. We'll take baby steps if we need to - no grand gestures necessary. Just the steady, sweet rhythm of self-compassion, woven into your daily jig. Now let's get to serenading our souls, shall we?

The Journey to Self-Acceptance

So you've been trying out all the bliss-boosting strategies from a breathing powerhouse to the sleep savvy lifestyle, and you just embarked on a voyage to the deepest realms of fabulous - you! Wait, are you telling me you're not quite feeling like a superstar in your own skin yet? No worries. Self-acceptance is less about rolling out the red carpet for your fabulousness and more about embracing the perfectly imperfect human gazing back in the mirror. Yup, that's right. It's giving yourself a high-five, quirks and all, because let's face it, those quirks are what make the symphony of you utterly original.

Imagine you're a painter, and life is this vast, vibrant canvas. Over the years, you've probably splattered it with a variety of hues - some you love, some you wish you could paint over. Self-acceptance is gazing at that canvas, acknowledging every stroke, and deciding to love the masterpiece you're becoming. It's no small feat, but who said anything worthwhile was ever easy?

Start by looking back (but no dwelling, promise?) at the previous chapters. You've laid the groundwork for a life sprinkled with joy like confetti at a parade. But it's instrumental to remember that no amount of meditation, healthy eats, or dreamy sleep can replace the magic of embracing who you are in this exact moment. No returns, no exchanges. This is the VIP edition of you.

Crucial as it is, the journey to self-acceptance is often lined with the temptation to self-criticize. It's like you're on this hike, right? You're aiming for the summit of Mount Self-Love, but then, boom - a wild negative thought appears. Instead of battling it, acknowledge its presence. Then, take a deep breath and let it pass like clouds on a windy day. You don't need that kind of baggage where you're headed.

Let's talk about your inner circle for a second—yes, those folks you vibe with. Their perceptions can influence how you see yourself, no doubt. But true self-acceptance? That's not a chorus; it's a solo act. It's about understanding you're complete, even if you're rolling solo on a Friday night with just Netflix for company. The key is to anchor your worth internally, not out there in the applause or critiques of the gallery.

Now, if your inner critic were a person, you'd probably have stopped inviting them to dinner a long time ago. Show yourself the same courtesy. Recognise the difference between constructive self-reflection and that nagging critic that just loves to party at your expense. Invite kindness to take a seat at the table instead, and you'll find that it's an excellent dining companion.

Always remember, your journey is as unique as your fingerprint. While your bestie might be leaps and bounds down the self-acceptance road, you might still be lacing up your sneakers. That's cool. There's no rush. This isn't about keeping pace with anyone else. It's about setting your own rhythm, so even if it's a samba one day and a waltz the next, you're dancing to the beat of your own drum.

But hey, let's be honest. The road to self-acceptance isn't paved with just sunshine and butterflies. There will be potholes - heck, maybe even a sinkhole or two. It's okay to stumble, to feel uncertain and vulnerable at times. These aren't signs that you're off track; they're proof of your humanness and your courage to keep moving forward.

Speaking of stumbles, don't forget the gold in your failures. They're not just oops moments; they're rich, fertile ground for growth. When you start seeing your missteps as opportunities to learn and not as the universe's way of punking you, you'll find it easier to accept yourself, blunders and all.

Another thing—the past is a nifty place with all its lessons and whatnot, but living there? Not so great. Self-acceptance is also about forgiving past you - yes, even for that cringy thing you did in high school - and giving yourself permission to move on. You aren't your past mistakes, and you surely aren't doomed to repeat them. You're a work in progress, and that's a beautiful place to be.

No talk of self-acceptance is complete without a shoutout to boundaries. They're not just there to keep people out; they're there to protect what's valuable - your peace, your energy, your authenticity. Create them, respect them, and watch how you begin to flourish in the space they hold for you.

And when you need a little backup in your self-acceptance quest, don't forget the power of affirmation. Sprinkle them around like pixie dust. A simple "I am enough" can do wonders when repeated with conviction and belief. Who knew a few words could pack such a punch?

You know that perfect version of yourself you sometimes dream about? Let's revise that fantasy because you're already the leading character in the most authentic story you could tell. Embrace that plot twist, will you?

Finally, celebrate the small victories. Toast to the day you smiled at your reflection without a hint of judgment or the moment you chose self-compassion over criticism. Those tiny victories aren't just stepping stones; they're the lifeblood of your journey to self-acceptance. Each one is a badge of honour, proof that you're on your way to becoming your own biggest fan. And honestly? There's nothing quite as blissful as being the hero of your own story.

Daily Practices for Self-Compassion

Have probably garnered your interest because they sound like a warm blanket on a rainy day, don't they? Well, they kinda are! But instead of a blanket, these practices are habits you weave into the fabric of your everyday life. Let's cast our gaze on self-compassion's greatest hits that you can perform as daily rituals.

First up, we've got the mirror pep talk. I get it if you're rolling your eyes, but hear me out. Every morning, while brushing your teeth or combing your hair, look yourself dead in the eye and say something positive and aloud, like, "Hey, you're doing the best you can, and that's pretty awesome." It may feel silly initially, but it's about setting the tone for your day with kindness—because you, my friend, deserve your kindness as much as anyone else does.

Then there's the art of the gentle 'no.' Often, we berate ourselves for not doing enough, so we say 'yes' when we want to say 'no.' Today, let's try saying 'no' to one thing that doesn't serve us, without an ounce of guilt. Guess what? The world won't collapse, and you'll have just scored some extra self-respect points.

On to mindfulness we march, and I promise it's not about touching your toes or twisting into a pretzel - unless that's your thing, of course. Mindfulness is about being present with whatever you're doing. Sipping coffee? Taste it. Walking to work? Feel your steps. It's about appreciating the now, which is a fabulous way to show yourself some love as you're giving yourself the gift of attention.

Pencil in some 'me time,' and I do mean literally. Mark it in your calendar as you would an important meeting because, let's face it, you're important too. Read a book, soak in the tub, dance to your favourite jam - whatever floats your boat. And during this time, let go of the 'shoulds' and embrace the 'wants.'

While we're on the topic, let's talk about the joy of jotting down thoughts. Keeping a journal isn't just for teenage angst; it's a sacred space for your thoughts and feelings. This act of pouring yourself onto paper is incredibly validating and, dare I say, therapeutic. So go ahead, spill the beans to your bound confidant.

Launch an offensive against the inner critic. We've all got one, and it loves to chatter. Whenever you hear that negative inner dialogue, challenge it. Ask, "Is this true, or is this just a rogue thought?" By scrutinising these thoughts, you'll often find they're about as substantial as a soap bubble.

Gratitude isn't just for Thanksgiving, and it's a staple food in the diet of self-compassion. Take a moment each day to reflect on something (or things) you're grateful for. Maybe it's the snugness of your socks or the smile from a stranger. These little things? They're big deals for cultivating a friendly relationship with life.

Then there's the ol' body scan meditation. Lay down, close your eyes, and mentally scan from the tips of your toes to the top of your head. It's like going on a mini vacation, except the destination is you. Treat your body with kindness, acknowledging any discomfort without judgment, just gentle awareness.

Earmark moments for celebration—yep, even the tiny victories. Did you reply to that one email you've been avoiding? Victory dance! Handled a tough call without turning into a stress monster? High five yourself! We're quick to criticise our mishaps but often forget to celebrate our wins, no matter their size.

When things feel overwhelming, it's time for the five-finger-breathing exercise. Hold up a hand and trace the outline with the index finger of your other hand, inhaling as you go up a finger, exhaling as you go down. It's a quirky little way to come back to your breath and calm the cardiac salsa in your chest.

Okay, let's talk self-compassion break, not to be confused with snacking—though snacks can be involved. This is about recognising a challenging moment, acknowledging that it's part of the human experience, and offering yourself some comfort. Maybe it's a walk, a piece of chocolate, or squeezing a stress ball into submission—whatever delivers that TLC you need.

Channelling kindness to others can also boomerang back to you. Toss a compliment like it's confetti because watching others light up can ignite your own sense of warmth. Being kind doesn't mean you become a doormat; it means you're spreading the self-compassion vibe, making it a win-win.

Establish boundaries like they're the hottest trend because, well, they are totally in vogue. Boundaries are the bouncers of your wellbeing, keeping the good stuff in and the not-so-good stuff out. When you respect your limits, you show yourself that your needs and feelings are valid and essential.

Lastly, weave in some creativity. Whether you're doodling during a conference call or throwing together an impromptu meal masterpiece, creativity is self-compassion's playful cousin. It invites spontaneity and joy into the mundane and is a refreshing way to express and validate yourself.

Remember, self-compassion is about being your own best friend. Some days are tougher, and the kind words may feel forced. That's okay. Keep at it, because practice doesn't make perfect - it makes progress. And before you know it, these practices will be as natural as breathing - something you do without even thinking twice about how essential it is to your very existence.

Chapter 11:
The Gratitude Attitude

Okay, so, turning to gratitude might feel a bit like your grandma's advice at Thanksgiving, "Count your blessings, dear." But let's be real, Grandma was onto something. Gratitude isn't just old school, it's life school. Imagine flipping the switch on your perspective, where setbacks become setups for greater joys, and the mundane glimmers with specks of awesome. It's like wearing those rose-tinted glasses, except you aren't deluding yourself - you're actually tuning into the truckload of good stuff that's already parked in your life's driveway.

Adopting a gratitude mindset doesn't mean you're ignoring the chaos of life; it's about choosing to dance in the rain rather than just getting drenched. Once you start noticing the little things - a piping hot coffee, a stranger's smile, or that perfectly timed green light - you're basically jump-starting a joyride for your soul. This juju isn't just feel-good fluff; it's backed by science. So, let's dive into turning "thanks" into a superpower and watch as the room gets brighter - if it's actually just the same ol' lamp.

Embracing Gratitude in Daily Life

Isn't some magical state of mind that's accessible only to those who practice yoga at sunrise or meditate by moonlight. Nope, it's for every one of us - even if your idea of spiritual awakening is hitting the snooze button the third time. This glorious sensation of thankfulness can be as much a part of daily life as your morning coffee or evening sitcom binge.

Let's be clear here, fostering gratitude is like flexing a muscle - and not in a 'pumping iron' kind of way that makes your face look like a constipated bulldog. It's more like a gentle stretch that slowly but surely increases your flexibility until one day, voila, you're touching your toes without a groan or a grimace.

So, you ask, how does one casually slip gratitude into their life like that extra slice of pizza you convince yourself you didn't eat? Here's a hint: it begins the moment you wake up. Before you plant your feet on the cold floor, take a second to be thankful that you can feel that chill - yep, unpleasant sensations count too because they mean you're alive and kicking!

And when you're sipping on that first glorious cup of caffeine laced with hope for a productive day, take a moment. Look at the steam rising in soft swirls, smell the richness. That's not just a cup of coffee; that's a sensory experience you're lucky to have, every single day.

As you go about your rat race, be it the commute, the office politics, or even standing in line at the grocery store, don't forget to find little specks of gold. Maybe it's a song on the radio that reminds you of a great time, or that the lettuce you picked up is remarkably fresh - small wins, folks.

Some days, gratitude is harder to summon than a smile when you burn dinner. On those days, go small. Be grateful for the roof over your head, for the food (yes, even the charred bits) that you can eat, for the people around you, even if right now they're the source of your burnt dinner frustration.

Scribbling in a gratitude journal might feel as passé as the pet rocks from the '70s, but trust me, it's worth a shot. A simple bullet list at the end of the day - stuff like 'sunshine', 'a friend's text', or 'finally nailed that TikTok dance move' - can act as your personal highlight reel.

Sharing your gratitude is as important as feeling it. Compliment someone, not in a cheeseball, 'you're as radiant as the light of a thousand suns' way, but sincerely. 'Hey, I noticed you did [insert kind deed].

Thanks, you're awesome!' can brighten both your worlds.

Let's talk about those tricky times - when nothing seems worth a thank you. Flip the switch; there's a lesson tucked away in every mishap. Maybe that flat tyre taught you resilience or introduced you to a new friend who helped you change it. That's gratitude wearing a sneaky disguise.

Gratitude shouldn't be a fair-weather friend; it's also for when skies are grey. When the storm rolls in, that's your cue. Be the person who's grateful for umbrellas, raincoats, or the chance to jump in puddles like a five-year-old. Because why not? Life's messy, be thankful for the washing machine.

Food isn't just for eating; it's an opportunity for gratitude. Indulge in a celebratory dance whenever you take a bite of something delicious. Just a little wiggle at the dinner table for how fortunate you are to have this tasty experience. Bonus: You'll entertain or utterly confuse your dining companions.

Practice saying 'thank you' like it's a secret spell that unlocks hearts and doors. Not a half-hearted mumble, but a genuine expression of appreciation, whether it's the barista who hands you your latte or the coworker who holds the elevator. Make it count.

On the more reflective evenings, consider the bigger picture. Think about the Earth spinning in space, the stars twinkling in the vast unknown, and the remarkable fact that you're part of this cosmic ballet. A little gratitude to the universe for letting you join the dance doesn't go amiss.

But hey, don't beat yourself up on the days when gratitude feels like a distant concept. Remember, it's a practice. Some days it's all about survival, and that's okay. There's something profoundly beautiful about recognising tomorrow is a fresh start, a new chance to spot life's little gems.

In the end, embracing gratitude in daily life is pretty much about staying awake to the wonders around you, both big and small. It's like choosing to wear those rose-coloured glasses, but instead of distorting reality, they clarify it, revealing all the beauty and kindness that's there just waiting to be acknowledged. So, let's fill our hearts to the brim, one thankful thought at a time - because when you do, life doesn't just feel good, it feels downright fabulous.

Expanding Joy Through Thankfulness

If the last section left you feeling as snug as a bug curled up with a cup of hot cocoa, then you're in the right headspace to expand on that warmth. Consider thankfulness as the secret sauce that takes your joy from delightful to downright euphoric. It's about painting your daily life in shades of gratitude, transforming the mundane into something extraordinary.

Think about it this way: when you're feeling grateful, it's like you're giving your brain a high-five. Science has shown that gratitude activates areas in the brain linked to the neurotransmitter dopamine—the feel-good juice. So, every time you express thankfulness, your brain gets a dollop of neurochemical sweetness.

But how exactly do you cultivate this habit of thankfulness? It's not like we find ourselves naturally beaming with gratitude while we're stuck in traffic or when the Wi-Fi cuts out. It's a matter of mindfulness, of flipping the script in your head from lack to abundance, from "ugh" to "oh wow!"

Start small—if you spy a friend sporting a smile, mentally chalk up a point of thanks. If your morning coffee tastes just right, silently send a shout-out to the universe for its cosmic barista skills. These mini moments of gratefulness set the stage for grander acts of appreciation.

Moving on, let's not forget the power of a gratitude journal. It sounds like an extra homework assignment, but trust me, it's the kind that makes you happier by the day. Scribble down three things you're thankful for each night before bed, and watch as a pattern of positivity starts to stitch itself into the fabric of your life.

Oh, and let's not just keep this gratitude party in our heads. Pass the vibe along! A thank you to the bus driver or a genuine compliment to a coworker amplifies the joy. What you'll find is a boomerang effect—the more good feelings you throw out into the world, the more come flying back at you.

Here's the kicker about thankfulness—it's contagious! Ever been around someone who's just so darn chipper you can't help but start seeing the silver linings too? That could be you, sparking joy wildfires wherever you roam. Just imagine being the catalyst for a chain reaction of smiles. Now, that's living.

Sure, there will be days when gratitude is as elusive as a Wi-Fi signal in the wilderness. The trick is to lean into even the tiniest of gratitudes. Like the fact that you even have a wilderness to wander in, or that the Wi-Fi will probably be back before you finish that hike.

As for the big stuff, remember that gratitude isn't reserved for milestones like promotions or birthdays. It's for the breath in your lungs, the sun that rises every day without fail, and the fact that pizza exists. Those constants are golden nuggets of joy waiting to be appreciated.

Moreover, embracing thankfulness helps us become more resilient. When life lobs lemons your way, rather than dodging, catch them and make some delectable lemonade. This mindset isn't about ignoring the sour; it's about finding the sweetness that's there too.

And don't just think of gratitude as a solo endeavour. Sharing your thankful thoughts can strengthen relationships. Acknowledge the blessings others bring into your life and watch the connection between you blossom. It's like telling life, "Hey, I see what you did there, and I like it!"

So, you've been sprinkling this thankfulness magic all over the place. Now what? It's time to take stock. Every now and then, reflect on how this practice has enriched your life. Bet you anything you'll find joy popping up in places you never expected, like whack-a-moles of happiness just waiting for you to take notice.

And hey, if you still need convincing, give it a try for a week. What's the worst that could happen? You'll end up with a week's worth of warm fuzzies and maybe even a new perspective on your day-to-day grind. In the realm of potential outcomes, those are pretty sweet.

The bottom line is, thankfulness doesn't have to be all Thanksgiving and grand gestures. It's about recognising the little victories, the everyday beauties, and the tiny acts of kindness that often go unnoticed. It's in the acknowledgment of these things where real joy expands like a balloon ready to soar.

Imagine thankfulness as your personal joy magnifying glass, bringing into focus the good that's constantly swirling around you. Get into the groove of gratitude, and you'll find that the melody of your life starts sounding a whole lot sweeter. So let's turn up the volume on that joy, one thank you at a time.

Chapter 12:
Do Not Worry, Be Happy

Coming off a high from channelling gratitude in Chapter 11, let's swing into the chill vibes of Chapter 12 with a smooth transition into nixing those pesky worries that keep us up at night. I'm talking about swapping stress for a pair of proverbial rose-coloured glasses—but don't worry; there's nothing impractical about this swap meet. In fact, it's all about grounding ourselves in the practicality of positivity. Recognising stressors isn't about pointing fingers or playing hide-and-seek with our fears. It's about opening our eyes, saying 'I see you' to what bothers us, and choosing to respond with a high five to happiness instead of a handshake with anxiety.

We're going to sift through the mental clutter with tools that are as handy as a Swiss Army knife in Bear Grylls' pocket. We'll equip ourselves with simple, yet potent, daily habits that help maintain an upbeat outlook. Because let's face it, everyone has moments that test their zen, but with this chapter, you're basically becoming the MacGyver of merriment, capable of defusing worry bombs with nothing more than an elastic band, a paperclip, and a wink. So, let's keep those worry monsters at bay and step into a world where 'Don't worry, be happy' isn't just a catchy tune—it's your new theme song. Ready? Let's turn the page and face those stress gremlins head-on with a smile that's contagious.

Recognising and Reducing Stressors

We've all been there: heart racing, palms sweating, and that pesky little vein in your forehead doing the cha-cha. Stress has this not-so-cute way of crashing into our lives, often when we least expect it. But have no fear, my enlightened accomplices in the pursuit of zen, for this chapter is all about spotting those sneaky stressors and giving them the boot before they crash your peace party.

First things first, let's play detective and track down what's actually winding you up. Stressors come in all shapes and sizes, from traffic jams to in-laws who think boundaries are just a suggestion. Sometimes we're so tangled up in survival mode, we don't even notice what's stressing us out until it's screaming in our faces – or we're screaming into a pillow. The trick? Start by keeping a stress diary. Jotting down when you feel on edge can reveal patterns and help you pinpoint the culprits. You might be surprised to find that it's not just significant life events but also the little daily hassles adding to your stress smoothie.

Once you've got your list, it's time to divide and conquer. Some stressors are like that gum on your shoe – annoyingly sticky and hard to remove. These are the ones you can't exactly change, like the relentless ticking of the clock or, yep, the weather. For those, you'll need to change up your reaction; more on that in a sec. The others, however, are like those subscription emails you never read – totally within your power to declutter. Goodbye, twice-daily sale alerts; hello, inbox nirvana!

Let's talk about tackling the stressors you can change. Peek at that diary. Is work popping up more than cat memes on your feed? Maybe it's time to chat with your boss about your workload, or to shut down your computer at a reasonable hour. Discover your limits, then draw a line thicker than the one at your favourite brunch place. Saying 'no' can be more powerful than any superfood elixir for your peace of mind.

But what about those unchangeable stressors? It's all about the art of acceptance and adaptation. Take a deep breath (we've all mastered those silky-smooth breathwork skills from Chapter 2, right?) and let go of trying to control the uncontrollable. It's like trying to teach a cat to fetch – futile and frustrating. Instead, focus on what you *can* do, such as giving yourself extra time to navigate through traffic jams or investing in some quality rain gear for those wet days.

And hey, understand this: stress isn't always the villain. Sometimes, it's the fire under your booty that gets you moving. But when stress morphs into a regular squatter in your life, it's time to usher it towards the exit. Stress management techniques such as meditation, detailed lovingly in Chapter 3, can help kick it to the curb.

Meditation not your jam? No worries. There's a galaxy of stress-reduction strategies out there. You could break a sweat in a dance class, belt out your favourite tunes, or sink into the sweet escape of a book. The key is to find your personal stress-buster that lights up your world like a pinball machine and stick with it.

Let's not forget the power of a good chuckle. Laughter can be a legit stress-reliever – it's like giving your insides a joyous little massage. Pop on a comedy, share a joke, or do something silly. Dance like a toddler or make faces in the mirror. It's hard to maintain a cortisol-fuelled frown when you're trying to outdo a five-year-old's dance moves.

Remember the golden rule of stress reduction: keep it simple, dear friends. Don't add more stress trying to become a stress-less sage. Pick one or two strategies and give them a shot. This isn't about building a stress-slaying fortress; it's about creating a tiny, peaceful oasis in the vast desert of life.

Now comes the part about those insidious little thoughts that speed our hearts without our permission. Yes, we're talking about the what-ifs, the worst-case scenarios, and the doomsday prophecies our brains love to concoct. It's like there's a miniature Spielberg in our minds, directing epic disaster movies. Cut! It's time to switch genres to something a little more chill. Techniques for reining in those runaway thoughts will get their close-up in Chapter 8.

Nourishment and sleep – ah, the sacred pillars of stress reduction. We've dived into the smorgasbord of diet tips in Chapter 5 and counted sheep in Chapter 6. Treating your body like the temple it is can arm it against stress. Imagine trying to joust with a pool noodle instead of a lance. That's stress without the backup of good food and sleep.

Social connection – let's not overlook this gem. Sharing your stress can actually dilute it, like adding water to overly strong coffee. Surround yourself with people who get you, who can lend an ear or offer a shoulder. Lean on your community, whether it's friends, family, or a bunch of lighthearted strangers in an origami club.

Lastly, sprinkle a little forward-thinking into your life. Stress loves to live in the now, making everything feel urgent and world-ending. But when you have a clear vision of where you're heading, courtesy of our dive into Discovering Purpose in Chapter 7, it's easier to see stressors for the temporary gremlins they are.

Now, don't you go thinking this is a one-time clean-up job. Reducing stress is a daily grind, or rather, a daily un-grind. Keep tweaking your stress-busting tactics as fervently as a barista perfecting their espresso. Stay vigilant, stay playful, and above all, stay kind to yourself. Remember, this journey you're on – it's a beautiful, messy, epic adventure. And you've got the tools to navigate it with a grace that would make Fred Astaire tip his hat.

With your stressors in check, we'll glide into our next rendezvous: *Practical Tools for Maintaining Positivity*. Because life is too short for perpetual frowns, and you, my friend, are too dazzling to let stress dim your shine. So, let's keep flipping through life's script with a pencil in hand, ready to rewrite those stress-filled scenes into moments of triumph.

Practical Tools for Maintaining Positivity

Ah, we've waded through the stress-soaked marshlands of worry and come out on the other side, ready for some clear skies and sunshine. Positivity isn't just a feeling; it's the very fabric we can use to tailor the everyday outfit of our lives. Let's kit ourselves out with some handy tools to keep those positive vibes flowing, shall we?

Maintaining a sunny outlook isn't all rainbows and butterflies; sometimes it's sticky like gum on the sidewalk. But hey, even gum has its flavour, right? So, our first tool on the list is a mental palate cleanser - mindfulness. You don't need to zen out under a Bonsai tree; mindfulness can be as simple as really tasting your morning coffee, feeling the suds on your hands when you wash dishes, or simply listening intently in conversations. Being present in the moment pushes those pesky gloomy thoughts about the past or future aside. Make it a habit, and you'll find yourself relishing the richness of the now.

Next up, let's talk affirmations. Yes, I can hear a few eyes rolling, but stick with me. The words we whisper to ourselves carry weight. Swap out the "I can'ts" with "I definitely can and watch how your inner dialogue starts to change the game. Do it with a little spunk - a dash of attitude - and watch those affirmations work like your own personal hype crew.

If you've ever felt like a plastic bag drifting through the wind (cue Katy Perry), planting your feet and setting routines can be your anchor. Whether it's a morning stretch, brewing a perfect cup of tea, or jotting down your goals for the day - consistency breeds comfort, and comfort is a VIP guest at the positivity party.

Let's not forget about laughter, the universal solvent of stress. Keep your favourite comedy clips handy, make a pact to smile at strangers, or even indulge in a good ol' session of laughter yoga - yep, it's a real thing. Lighten up your day, intentionally seek humour, and giggle your way to positivity.

Diving deeper, gratitude is like the hot sauce of life. It adds a kick to everything. Try a gratitude journal, or make it a dinner-time tradition to share one thing you're thankful for. But let's keep it zesty - showing gratitude for the strange, the mundane, and even the lessons from the tough stuff can turn the volume up on positivity.

Here's a nifty one - visualisation. Instead of daydreaming about your celebrity crush (which is totally fine, by the way), visualise your best life. Paint your aspirations in bright colours in your mind's gallery. This mental rehearsal primes your brain to spot opportunities and bright sides like an expert.

Boy, we can't skip over music! Create a playlist that's like a personal soundtrack for those feel-good montages of your life. Need a pep talk? Blast those anthems. Music is a direct line to our emotions, so cue up DJ Positive and let the good times roll.

Surround yourself with positive reinforcements, and I'm not just talking about Post-It notes with smiley faces, although those are cute too. Cultivate relationships with people who lift you up, challenge you constructively, and aren't afraid to dance in the rain with you - metaphorically or literally.

Keep a keen eye on your media diet. Just like a night of bingeing on junk food can leave you with a stomach ache, doomscrolling can leave your positivity queasy. Balance your intake with news that's uplifting, and sprinkle your social media feed with accounts that inspire and make you feel good about yourself and the world.

Not every day is going to be a winner, and that's okay. On the raincloud days, practice gentle self-compassion. Talk to yourself like you would a dear friend - with kindness, understanding, and maybe a scoop of ice cream. Because let's face it, ice cream is the spoonful of sugar that makes the medicine go down.

Lifelong learning keeps your mind engaged and optimistic. Learn a language, pick up an instrument, or dive into a new book. Stretching those intellectual muscles can provide a refreshing mental escape and remind you of the wonderment that surrounds us. Get curious, keep growing, and positivity will follow.

Foster flexibility in your thinking. Life throws curveballs, and while we can't always knock 'em out of the park, we can learn to dodge, weave, and even catch a few. Approach challenges with a 'how can I make the best of this' attitude. Flexibility is a key player on team positivity.

Decluttering your space is like decluttering your mind. Tackle that closet, sort through those old emails, and create a sanctuary that reflects the calm, positive oasis you want inside your head. A clear space equals a clear mind; it's like feng shui for your brain.

Last but not least, savour the small wins. Celebrate every step forward, from not hitting the snooze button to finishing that big project. Revel in them, dance a little celebration jig, because success, no matter the size, is positivity fuel.

There we have it - a toolbox brimming with practical instruments to maintain that positive flow. Consider this your personal positivity workshop where you tinker, experiment, and customise these tools to fit

The Blueprint for Bliss

into the unique design of your life. And what's exciting is that these tools don't rust; they get shinier with use. So keep at it, get creative, and let that positivity shine!

Chapter 13:
Living the Blueprint for Bliss

Sifting through the preceding chapters, you've armed yourself with a powerhouse of strategies for a blissful existence. You're not just walking the path; you've become the path, the architect of your joy and well-being. So now, let's talk about stitching these patches of wisdom into the quilt of your daily life.

You began this journey by laying a foundation, understanding that bliss isn't a magical destination but a blueprint for living. Let's be real, life throws curveballs, but recalling the unifying principles of science and spirituality, remember it's all about how you swing the bat.

Maybe you've found your breathwork groove, in through the nose, out through the mouth, harnessing calm amidst chaos. It's funny how something as simple as breathing can steer the ship through stormy waters to serene seas, right?

Oh, and that meditation practice? Whether it's five minutes or an hour of finding your Zen, you're essentially giving your mind the spa treatment it deserves. Keep at it; cultivating that inner peace is a game-changer!

Our health check reminded you that listening to your body is not just polite; it's crucial. Just as an orchestra tunes their instruments, you've learned to fine-tune your physical, emotional, and spiritual well-being for a harmonious symphony.

Let's not forget the food on your plate! Nourishing your body with a blissful diet is like fuelling a rocket ship – you want premium fuel for that stellar journey. Remember, every bite is a vote for how you want to feel and function.

Sleep, once an underrated headliner, now takes centre stage. With your sleep hygiene dialled in, those zzz's have become a superpower, because after all, who doesn't want to wake up feeling like a superhero?

Discovering your purpose was like digging for buried treasure, and guess what? You struck gold! Aligning what you do with who you are turns every day into a work of art. Keep painting that masterpiece of yours.

Those pesky subconscious beliefs? You've been rewiring them like a pro electrician, flipping the switches that illuminate your potential and dimming the ones that were dulling your sparkle.

Integrating body, mind, and spirit has set you on a trajectory toward holistic balance. You've been mixing these parts with the finesse of a master chef, whipping up a gourmet life experience that's as rich as it is fulfilling.

Self-love, once a foreign concept to some, is now your tender daily practice. It's the comfy sweater you wear, warming your spirit with soft threads of self-compassion and kindness.

Gratitude, more than a simple thank-you, has become your force field. It transforms ordinary moments into extraordinary ones, and even on mundane Mondays, you find reasons to celebrate.

Remember stressing over small stuff? Now you're the cool cat, unfazed by life's litter. With the tools to maintain positivity, your laughter comes easier, and worries have taken the backseat (if they even make it into the car).

So here you are. Living the blueprint for bliss isn't a secret formula; it's the artful application of what you now know and treasure. It's the rich tapestry you weave every day with threads of wisdom and practices of purpose.

Closure is just a myth in the world of personal growth. You're constantly evolving, always learning. And while this book concludes, your adventure continues with every sunrise. So, embrace your blueprint, cherish the journey, and live your bliss. Your best life is not a place to arrive at but a manner of travelling, and you, my friend, travel well.

About the Author

Richard Gibson is a Life, Relationships and Dating Coach in South Australia. His journey to becoming a life coach began after he experienced a difficult period in his life and refused to give up.

Through his journey back to a place of strength and happiness, he gained extensive knowledge in the area of personal development. He found a new purpose in life - service to others. This led him to become a Life Coach, and he now has a passion for inspiring others to live the life they deserve.

If you're interested in learning more about Life Coaching or getting in touch with Richard, you can visit his website at **www.primaryself.com**.

Appendix

Alright, you've danced through the chapters, sidestepped your way through self-discovery, meditated on the mesmeric musings about life, and, let's be real, you've become a bit of a bliss-seeking ninja. But as we all know, the quest for knowledge never really stops, does it? This Appendix isn't just a back-of-the-book thought. Oh no! It's like that secret level in your favourite video game - loaded with cheat codes and power-ups, except here, they're resources that'll boost your journey to living your absolute best life.

Recommended Reading and Material Now that you've snaked your way through the mental jungle gym this book provides, it's time to talk about some sustenance for the adventurous soul. Knowledge is the new kale, after all, and I've curated a list of brain-nourishing treats that will keep you flexing those cognitive muscles long after you've closed the last page of this literary expedition.

"The Untethered Soul: The Journey Beyond Yourself" by Michael A. Singer:

Overview: "The Untethered Soul" offers profound insights into self-discovery, inner peace, and personal transformation. Written by spiritual teacher Michael A. Singer, this book invites readers to explore their consciousness, break free from limitations, and embrace the present moment.

Key Themes: Inner Exploration: Singer delves into our relationship with thoughts, emotions, and energy patterns. He encourages us to understand the source of our inner energy fluctuations.

Freedom from Limitations: By practising mindfulness and meditation, we can release painful memories and habitual thought patterns that hinder our happiness.

Holistic Approach: The book emphasises not only external actions but also inner well-being, self-love, and emotional balance.

Impact: Readers find clarity and practical guidance on their spiritual journey.

Singer's simple language and relatable examples make spirituality accessible.

In summary, "The Untethered Soul" is a transformative read that empowers us to live authentically and let go of what holds us back.

"Think Like a Monk" by **Jay Shetty**:

Overview: In this transformative book, Jay Shetty - social media superstar and former monk - distils timeless wisdom into practical steps for daily life. "Think Like a Monk" invites readers to cultivate peace, purpose, and mindfulness in a world filled with distractions.

Key Takeaways:

Overcoming Negativity: Learn how to shift your mindset and overcome negative thoughts.

Breaking the Overthinking Cycle: Discover techniques to stop overthinking and find clarity.

Embracing Fear: Understand how fear can be a powerful teacher.

Seeking Happiness Within: Realize that happiness isn't found externally; it's an inner journey.

Learning from Others: Every encounter offers a lesson; be open to learning from everyone.

Finding Purpose: Explore your purpose beyond societal expectations.

Kindness and Success: Kindness is a crucial ingredient for a successful life.

Why Read It?:

Jay Shetty draws from his monk experience to provide actionable steps. The book offers practical tools for reducing stress and improving well-being.

It encourages readers to think differently and live intentionally.
In a world of chaos, "Think Like a Monk" guides us toward inner peace and purpose.

"You Are the Placebo: Making Your Mind Matter" by **Dr. Joe Dispenza**:

Overview: In this thought-provoking book, Dr. Joe Dispenza explores the fascinating concept of the placebo effect. He delves into how our beliefs and thoughts can profoundly impact our health and well-being.

Key Insights:

Mind-Body Connection: Dr. Dispenza shares documented cases of individuals who reversed serious illnesses - such as cancer, heart disease, and depression - solely through the power of belief.

The Placebo Effect: Learn how belief can influence physical healing, even without external substances like drugs or surgery.

Scientific Evidence: The book combines neuroscience, psychology, and quantum physics to describe the workings of the placebo effect.

Why Read It?:

If you're curious about the mind's influence on health, this book offers eye-opening stories and practical insights.

Dr. Dispenza's approach encourages us to harness our mental power for positive transformation.

In a world where our thoughts shape our reality, "You Are the Placebo" invites us to explore the untapped potential within.

"The Surrender Experiment: My Journey into Life's Perfection" by **Michael A. Singer**:

Overview:

In this thought-provoking memoir, Michael A. Singer—author of "The Untethered Soul"—shares his remarkable journey toward enlightenment.

The book explores the magic that unfolds when we surrender to life's flow and let go of control.

Key Themes:

Surrender: Singer narrates how surrendering to life's unfolding events led to unexpected opportunities and personal growth.

Harmony: The book emphasises finding harmony amidst life's chaos by releasing resistance.

Spiritual Lessons: Singer combines personal anecdotes with spiritual insights, offering a roadmap to perpetual happiness.

Impact:

Readers gain inspiration to release conflicting beliefs, worries, and misdirected desires.

The memoir encourages living in the present moment and embracing life's perfection.

In a world filled with noise, "The Surrender Experiment" invites us to trust the unfolding journey.

Resources for Continued Growth

Well, pat yourself on the back because you've just journeyed through the crème de la crème of living your best life. But hold on, the party isn't over yet. Imagine your personal growth as a garden—you've planted some stellar seeds, and now it's time to nurture them. Your brain's ready to soak in even more sunshine and your soul, well, it's just getting started!

Think of resources for continued growth as the water, fertiliser, and golden sunshine your internal garden craves. They come in various forms: books, podcasts, seminars, courses, and the unconditional love of an enthusiastic dog that missed you while you were out. Yes, even Fido is here to teach you about unconditional love and being present!

Books are like the best friends who never get tired of repeating the same wise stories. They sit on your shelf, patiently waiting for when you need them. So, keep a library that inspires you. Surround yourself with pages that push you to greater heights and words that whisper sweet affirmations of your limitless potential. Don't just limit yourself to non-fiction; fiction can offer profound lessons in the guise of a good story too!

Podcasts are your portable professors, offering lectures in the university of life right in your pocket. Whether you're cooking up a storm or sweating it out on the treadmill, let these audio gems offer you insights and companionship. Choose topics that resonate with you, stir your curiosity, and tickle your brain cells in all the right ways.

In the mood for some face-to-face wisdom sharing? Seminars and workshops are your jam. These are places where you'll meet fellow adventurers on the bliss-seeking trail. Together, you'll dive deep, and share aha-moments so powerful, they'll send shivers right down to your toes. The connections you make here can become part of your support system as you continue to grow.

If you're the high-flier who loves a structured approach to soaring new heights, then courses could be your takeoff runway. Online platforms are offering courses in everything from quantum physics to basket weaving these days, so you're bound to find something that matches your quest for knowledge. Just remember, finishing a course is like scoring a point in the game of life – it's a celebration, not a chore.

Let's not forget the daily dose of "aha!" that comes from journaling. Scribble your insights, doodle your dreams, jot down your joys; your journal is the most patient listener. Plus, it's fascinating to look back and see how much you've grown. It's like high-fiving your past self for being so insightful!

Remember, the internet is a treasure trove of resources - blogs, videos, online communities, and more. Sure, there's some weird stuff out there, but the gold you'll find is worth the digital excavation. Be selective, though; not every shiny object is worth your click.

Connecting with mentors and coaches can be life-changing. These are the Yodas to your Luke Skywalker, the Mr. Miyagis to your Daniel-san. Seek out those who resonate with your values and have walked the path before you. Their wisdom can help you navigate the trickiest parts of your journey.

This is my opportunity to shamelessly plug my life coaching services. If you understand the principles in this book but struggle to apply them or need some accountability, visit www.primaryself.com to book a coaching session with me.

There's no need to go at it alone, so get involved with community groups or clubs that share your interests. It's like finding your tribe and doing the happy dance together in a circle. You'll uplift one another, provide support, and share the kind of laughter that echoes in your memory for years to come.

If you're thinking, "But what if I fall out of the growth wagon?" Fear not! Subscription services – like monthly book clubs or meditation app memberships – can give you that gentle nudge you need to stay on track. It's like having a friendly ghost of growth reminding you to keep at it.

Experiential learning is also a treasure. Travel, volunteer, step out of your comfort zone. These experiences have a way of teaching you lessons that stick like gooey gum under a school desk—annoyingly persistent and strikingly memorable. The world is your classroom with an endless supply of electives.

Lastly, don't forget the most important resource: your fellow human beings. Engage in deep conversations, exchange ideas, listen to heartbeats, and stories. Every person you meet is a living library, each with their unique set of tales to tell.

As your arsenal of resources for growth expands, remember to be discerning. You're the DJ of your personal development playlist, so mix in only the tracks that get your soul grooving.

Stay hungry for growth, stay foolish enough to believe you can make a difference, and stay equipped with the very best tools this life has to offer. Armed with these resources, your journey for continued growth is not just about crossing finish lines—it's about cherishing every stride, leap, and sometimes, the epic wipeouts.

So as you close one book (figuratively and literally), open another, tune into a new podcast, or step onto the mat for another sunrise yoga session, embrace these resources for what they are—fuel for your ever-burning fire of curiosity and passion for life.

Keep learning, keep laughing, and keep loving the process of becoming the best possible you. After all, as long as you're soaking up the good stuff, your garden of growth will thrive in ways you've only imagined. Onward and upward, my friend!

www.ingramcontent.com/pod-product-compliance
Lightning Source LLC
Chambersburg PA
CBHW031420290426
44110CB00011B/466